A MAJOR LITERARY EVENT!

The publication of this new translation of
Kafka's *THE METAMORPHOSIS*—one of the
most widely read works of the twentieth century—is a milestone in publishing. This volume
contains not only a new translation but also
copious notes, letters and a wide selection of
critical essays off the beaten track.

"The acts of Kafka's real history are his stories
and novels, which are at the same time reflections on the act of writing itself. They are, of
course, reflections of something else besides—of
the cruelty of the family, the coldness of bureaucracy, the misery of cities. But this something else
becomes something less if it deprives us of the
most intense and coherent experience of Kafka's
world. At the center of this world are the feelings of isolation, indebtedness, and shortcoming
which mark his existence as a writer—that form
of estrangement that tries to maintain itself as
estrangement and to take this condition to its
limit. Kafka's stories treat questions of personal
happiness, social justice, and filial piety from the
standpoint of his fate as literature."
        —from the Introduction by Stanley Corngold

BANTAM LITERATURE

THE
METAMORPHOSIS

By Franz Kafka

Translated and Edited
by Stanley Corngold

BANTAM BOOKS · TORONTO · LONDON · NEW YORK

THE METAMORPHOSIS

A Bantam Book | March 1972

2nd printing ..	December 1972	7th printing .	November 1976
3rd printing	August 1973	8th printing	October 1977
4th printing	June 1974	9th printing	January 1979
5th printing	May 1975	10th printing	July 1979
6th printing	February 1976	11th printing	June 1980

COPYRIGHT AND ACKNOWLEDGMENTS

The copyright notices are listed below and on page v which constitutes an extension of this copyright page.

Extract from **The Trial** by Franz Kafka. Translated by Willa and Edwin Muir, revised and with additional materials translated by E. M. Butler. Copyright 1937, © 1956 by Alfred A. Knopf, Inc., and reprinted with their permission.

Letter by Franz Kafka to Max Brod, October 8, 1912, from Franz Kafka: A Biography by Max Brod. Copyright © 1960 by Schocken Books, Inc., and reprinted with their permission.

Walter Sokel's comments on Kafka's letter to Max Brod, October 8, 1912. Reprinted by permission of Albert Langen Georg Müller Verlag, GmbH, Munich.

Two conversations between Kafka and Gustav Janouch from Conversations With Kafka by Gustav Janouch. Translated by Goronwy Rees. Copyright © 1968 by S. Fisher Verlag, GmbH, Frankfurt am Main; translation © 1971 by S. Fischer Verlag, GmbH, Frankfurt am Main. Reprinted by permission of New Directions Publishing Corporation.

"Kafka to His Father," from Dearest Father by Franz Kafka. Translated by Ernst Kaiser and Eithne Wilkins. Copyright © 1954 by Schocken Books, Inc., and reprinted with their permission.

Entries in Kafka's Diaries from Diaries: 1910–1913 and Diaries: 1914–1923 by Franz Kafka. Diaries: 1910–1913 translated by Joseph Kresh. Copyright 1948 by Schocken Books, Inc., and reprinted with their permission. Diaries: 1914–1923 translated by Martin Greenberg. Copyright 1949 by Schocken Books, Inc., and reprinted with their permission.

Excerpt from Franz Kafka by Wilhelm Emrich. Translated by Sheema Z. Buehne. Copyright © 1968 by Frederick Ungar Publishing Company, Inc., and reprinted with their permission.

Excerpt from "Kafka's Obscurity: The Illusion of Logic in Narrative," by Ralph Freedman. From Modern Fiction Studies. Spring, 1962, Vol. VIII, No. 1. Copyright © 1962 by Purdue Research Foundation, Lafayette, Indiana, and reprinted with their permission.

"The Making of Allegory," by Edwin Honig. From his Dark Conceit. Copyright © 1959 by Edwin Honig. Reprinted by permission of Oxford University Press.

"Kafka's Conception of Being," by Max Bense from Kafka's Theory. Copyright 1952 by Verlag Kiepenheuer & Witsch, Cologne.

"Kafka's Fantasy of Punishment," by Hellmuth Kaiser from Franz Kafka's Inferno in IMAGO XVII, 1931. Copyright 1931 by Internationaler Psychonanalytischer Verlag. Reprinted by permission of Sigmund Freud Copyrights, London.

Extracts from "Franz Kafka's The Metamorphosis as Death and Resurrection Fantasy," by Peter Dow Webster. From AMERICAN IMAGO, XVI. Copyright © 1959 by American Imago. Reprinted by permission of Dr. George B. Wilber.

Excerpt from Franz Kafka, Tragik und Ironie by Walter Sokel. Reprinted by permission of Albert Langen Georg Müller Verlag, GmbH, Munich.

"The Writer Franz Kafka," and "Kafka the Artist," by Friedrich Beissner. Reprinted by permission of W. Kohlhammer Verlag, GmbH, Stuttgart.

Excerpt from Franz Kafka—Work and Project by Hellmut Richter. Reprinted by permission of Verlag Rütten & Loening, Berlin.

ISBN 0-553-14308-5

Bantam Books are published by Bantam Books, Inc. Its trademark, consisting of the words "Bantam Books" and the portrayal of a bantam, is Registered in U.S. Patent and Trademark Office and in other countries. Marca Registrada. Bantam Books, Inc., 666 Fifth Avenue, New York, New York 10019.

PRINTED IN THE UNITED STATES OF AMERICA

20 19 18 17 16 15 14 13 12 11

I am indebted to Allen Mandelbaum for proposing this book, and to Gregory Armstrong, its exemplary editor.

I wish to thank Ralph Freedman, Barney Milstein, and Ruth Hein for making valuable improvements to the translation. The Reference Division of the Princeton University Library helped me compile the bibliography.

Contents

Introduction

While he lived, Franz Kafka was an obscure writer of short novels; when he died, he became the body of works that has created our modern awareness. The metamorphosis of history by Kafka, and of Kafka by his art, is the most dramatic evidence of the power of literature since the Romantic movement.

During his lifetime Kafka published only five slim volumes of prose. *Meditation*, a collection of prose sketches reminiscent of Joyce's *Dubliners*, appeared in 1912, followed in 1913 by *The Stoker, A Fragment*, which we know today as the first chapter of the novel *Amerika*. *The Metamorphosis* was first published in November, 1915, scant months before *The Judgment*, the short work which Kafka considered as marking a breakthrough into his mature style. Toward the end of his life there appeared *In the Penal Colony* (1919), a harrowing meditation on torture and justice, and *A Country Doctor* (1920), a visionary tale of estrangement. Only a few of Kafka's friends knew during his lifetime that Kafka was also at work on the great novels which today form the basis for his reputation—*Amerika, The Trial, The Castle*.

Shortly before his death from tuberculosis in 1924, Kafka wrote a note to his friend, the novelist Max Brod, asking that all his papers, including the manuscripts of the novels, be burned. Brod chose to disregard Kafka's wish: he defended his decision on the ground that Kafka had made his last behest of a man who, he knew, would never consent to destroy his work. The result was that Kafka's novels, though none of them is quite finished, were published in Germany in the late 1920's. They disappeared from view in Germany during the Nazi period, but by then they had been translated and published in

Paris, London, and New York; and there, especially during the 1940's, the truthfulness and beauty of Kafka's work, its logic and bewitchment, began to preoccupy critics and interpreters. Kafka's prestige has steadily increased, so that today it would require a lifetime to study and master the critical literature that has grown up around his work.

Kafka was born in 1883 in Prague, then the capital of a province of the Austro-Hungarian Empire. He was born the citizen of a crumbling state, a German-speaker among Czech-speakers, a Jew among Gentiles—and in himself the loneliest of men. Within his family, dominated by his father Herrmann Kafka, a huge, selfish, overbearing businessman, Franz, the only son, lived a life of estrangement in a freezing solitude he called "Russian." He did not live alone until he was thirty-three; and he did not live with a woman until the last year of his life, when he fled Prague for Berlin. His poverty and the cold of winter in inflation-ridden Germany exacerbated his disease, and he died at the age of forty-one.

Kafka's life is almost empty of incident, apart from his two engagements to Felice Bauer, both of which he broke off. He does not appear to have had formative experiences; he did not make extensive trips or form associations with writers of equal stature. He attended a "good" German-language *Gymnasium* and studied literature briefly at the University of Prague before turning to law. Soon after obtaining his doctoral degree, he took up a position at the state Worker's Accident Insurance Institute, where he stayed until illness forced his retirement. He was a conscientious employee, rising to a position of considerable responsibility. He suffered, however, from the routine and stress of the office, for they interfered with the activity that mattered most—indeed, almost exclusively—to him: his nocturnal writing. He wrote in 1912:

It is easy to recognize a concentration in me of all my forces on writing. When it became clear in my organism that writing was the most productive direction for my being to take, everything rushed in that direction and left empty all those abilities which were directed toward the joys of sex, eating, drinking, philosophical reflection and above all music. . . . Naturally, I did not find this purpose independently and consciously, it found itself, and is now interfered with only by the office, but that interferes with it completely. . . . My development is now complete and, so far as I can see, there is nothing left to sacrifice; I need only throw my work in the office out of this complex in order to begin my real life.[*]

But the matter is more complicated. The *Diaries* go on to record periods of freedom from the office, yet no work accomplished. Kafka cared so much about his writing, felt so intensely its power over him, that he must have wanted to put up resistances to it for fear that it would leave nothing of himself.

Kafka's real history is his life as literature. To understand him we should substitute the word *literature* for the word *history* in R. G. Collingwood's formula: "History is the life of mind itself which is not mind except so far as it both lives in the historical process and knows itself as so living." The acts of Kafka's real history are his stories and novels, which are at the same time reflections on the act of writing itself. They are, of course, reflections of something else besides—of the cruelty of the family, the coldness of bureaucracy, the misery of cities. But this something else becomes something less if it deprives us of the most intense and coherent experience of Kafka's world. At the center of this world are the feelings of isolation, indebtedness, and shortcoming which mark his existence as a writer—that form of estrangement that tries to maintain itself as estrangement and to take this condition to its limit. Kafka's stories treat questions of personal happiness, social justice, and filial piety from the standpoint of his fate as literature.

---

[*] *The Diaries of Franz Kafka, 1910–1913*, ed. Max Brod, trans. Joseph Kresh (New York: Schocken Books, 1949), p. 211.

On the night of September 23, 1912, in a single sitting, Kafka composed the story *The Judgment*. He then noted in his *Diaries*, with a fine elation: "How everything can be said, how for everything, for the strangest fancies, there waits a great fire in which they perish and rise up again. . . . Only *in this way* can writing be done, only with such coherence, with such a complete opening out of the body and the soul." * What, besides the concentrated exercise of his faculties, can have led to such ecstasy?

The Judgment concerns a young businessman, Georg Bendemann, with whom Kafka afterward identified his own bourgeois personality. Georg is about to marry a young woman; and her initials, F. B., are those of the woman Kafka was thinking of marrying. Georg must write this news to a friend who lives in exile, in Russia, but he cannot do so, it appears, without either offending his friend or betraying his fiancée. For in his bitter and unproductive solitude his friend might only envy Georg's happiness and consider an invitation to return for the wedding as a judgment of the failure of his Russian venture. On the other hand, Georg owes it to his fiancée to make a straightforward declaration of his happiness to his friend. Georg finds a compromise, but his letter tells lies in favor of his fiancée, so that Georg must admit, after all, that he cannot tailor himself to his friend's pattern.

The second half of the story is visionary—impossible, really, to describe. This difficulty comes from the fact that the action is itself an unsettled combat between opposing points of view about what is taking place. Georg enters his father's room at the back of the apartment; the old man has been neglected and seems wretched and pitiable. Yet in the course of a few pages the perspective shifts decisively; the old man is changed from a feeble clown wearing soiled underwear into a haughty giant who reveals the news that it is he, not his son

---

* *Diaries, 1910–1913*, p. 276.

Georg, who really has a friend in Russia. Now the father rises up in bed to his full stature; and after accusing his son of an obscure fault, "radiant with insight," he proceeds to sentence him to death. Georg obeys. With a last display of the nimbleness which had always delighted his parents, and with the fleeting thought that he has always loved them, he leaps to his death by drowning. What is the meaning of this bizarre happiness which accompanies the execution of the most terrible fantasy thinkable?

Everything depends on the identification of the figure of the Russian friend with the life Kafka called "literature." Like the friend, Kafka would, as a writer, be condemned to bachelorhood and isolation. And in view of the intrinsic shortcoming of writing—for it cannot contain or create life—he would suffer a continual sense of poverty. Other details further this identification: Georg's relationship to his friend is based on writing (letters); like Kafka's writing, the friend's attempts at business have been failing; finally, the friend is described at the close of the story as something like an unpublished manuscript, as "yellow enough to be thrown away."

When Georg chooses to stay engaged to his fiancée rather than keep faith with his friend, the narrator of the story, whose point of view is very nearly identical with Georg's, faces a crisis. Breaking faith with literature, how can he continue? He proceeds, in a perspective distorted by anxiety, to envision the father. This is a necessary act, for the son, too, is now embarked on family life. But the surreality of the story suggests the loss of even fictional coherence; we are entering a world of sheer hypothesis. What follows must not in fact happen; the world depicted is the world as it must not be. The father reveals himself to be the true father of the Russian friend, the writer. If Kafka is now to grasp the life of literature as sponsored by the father, as his "ideal" offspring, then writing is only a neurotic reaction to the vitality of the father. Writing cannot be preferred to marriage. The decision to marry becomes inescapable

at the same time that it becomes worthless, for this is the
institution which perpetuates neurosis. Georg cannot
turn anywhere and escape guilt: guilt toward the fiancée,
guilt toward the friend, and worse, the knowledge that
this guilt is itself nothing—a contingent and not an essential concern of the self. If this is the case, then Kafka
has been sentenced to death.

The Judgment liberated in Kafka the insight essential
to his life: he must not betray his writing, either by
marrying or by supposing that his father is the source
and goal of his art. Through the story, this insight comes
into being with such force that Kafka afterward likened
it to "a regular birth, [which came out of me] covered
with filth and slime." * This image cannot fail to remind
the reader of the strange birth which is the subject of
Kafka's next story—the monstrous hero of *The Metamorphosis,* trailing filth and slime through the household of
his family. †

Now it would seem an extraordinary idea to claim that
Gregor Samsa, the vermin, literally expresses the condition of being a writer. It is possible that the obscurity
and irrevocableness of Gregor's sentence describes Kafka's
fate as a writer. But what connection can there be between a vermin image and the activity of writing?

The link is provided by an early story called "Wedding
Preparations in the Country" (1907), which portrays an
autonomous self through the figure of a beetle. Raban,
the hero, discovers an effortless way to arrange his marriage:

"And besides, can't I do it the way I always used to as a
child in matters that were dangerous? I don't even need
to go to the country myself, it isn't necessary. I'll send my
clothed body. If it staggers out of the door of my room,
the staggering will indicate not fear but its nothingness.
Nor is it a sign of excitement if it stumbles on the stairs,

---

* *Diaries, 1910–1913,* p. 278.
† My discussion of *The Judgment* is indebted to Martin Green-
berg's analysis of this story in his profound study, *The Terror of Art,
Kafka and Modern Literature* (New York: Basic Books, 1968).

if it travels into the country, sobbing as it goes, and there eats its supper in tears. For I myself am meanwhile lying in my bed, smoothly covered over with the yellow-brown blanket, exposed to the breeze that is wafted through that seldom aired room. The carriages and people in the street move and walk hesitantly on shining ground, for I am still dreaming. Coachmen and pedestrians are shy, and every step they want to advance they ask as a favor from me, by looking at me. I encourage them and encounter no obstacle.

"As I lie in bed I assume the shape of a big beetle, a stag beetle or a cockchafer, I think. [. . .]

"The form of a large beetle, yes. Then I would pretend it was a matter of hibernating, and I would press my little legs to my bulging belly. And I would whisper a few words, instructions to my sad body, which stands close beside me, bent. Soon I shall have done—it bows, it goes swiftly, and it will manage everything efficiently while I rest." *

This beetle's dreamy magnificence corresponds to Kafka's naive idea, before the fall of 1912, about his literary destiny. He saw it as the source of power and perfection:

The special nature of my inspiration . . . is such that I can do everything, and not only what is directed to a definite piece of work. When I arbitrarily write a single sentence, for instance, "He looked out of the window," it already has perfection.†

My happiness, my abilities, and every possibility of being useful in any way have always been in the literary field. And here I have, to be sure, experienced states . . . in which I completely dwelt in every idea, but also filled every idea, and in which I not only felt myself at my boundary, but at the boundary of the human in general.‡

The movement from the beautiful beetle Raban to the odious vermin Gregor marks Kafka's increasing aware-

* *Dearest Father: Stories and Other Writings*, trans. Ernst Kaiser and Eithne Wilkins (New York, 1954), pp. 6–7.
† *Diaries, 1910–1913*, p. 45.
‡ *Diaries, 1910–1913*, p. 58.

ness of the sacrifice that literature demands and the sense that writing does not lead necessarily to expansive states but to a kind of living death. Kafka's diary entry for August 6, 1914, reads:

> What will be my fate as a writer is very simple. My talent for portraying my dreamlike inner life has thrust all other matters into the background; my life has dwindled dreadfully, nor will it cease to dwindle. Nothing else will ever satisfy me. But the strength I can muster for that portrayal is not to be counted upon: perhaps it has already vanished forever, perhaps it will come back to me again, although the circumstances of my life don't favor its return. Thus I waver, continually fly to the summit of the mountain, but then fall back in a moment. Others waver too, but in lower regions, with greater strength; if they are in danger of falling, they are caught up by the kinsman who walks beside them for that very purpose. But I waver on the heights; it is not death, alas, but the eternal torments of dying.*

The precariousness of literature is the subject of a letter written to Max Brod in 1922:

> But what is it to be a writer? Writing is a sweet, wonderful reward, but its price? During the night the answer was transparently clear to me: it is the reward for service to the devil. This descent to the dark powers, this unbinding of spirits by nature bound, dubious embraces and whatever else may go on below, of which one no longer knows anything above ground, when in the sunlight one writes stories. Perhaps there is another kind of writing, I only know this one, in the night, when anxiety does not let me sleep, I only know this one. And what is devilish in it seems to me quite clear. It is the vanity and the craving for enjoyment, which is forever whirring around oneself or even around someone else . . . and enjoying it. The wish that a naive person sometimes has: "I would like to die and watch the others crying over

---

* *The Diaries of Franz Kafka, 1914–1923*, ed. Max Brod, trans. Martin Greenberg (New York, 1949), p. 77.

me," is what such a writer constantly experiences: he dies (or he does not live) and continually cries over himself.*

To be a writer is to know the delight of reflection and the beautiful lament, but it is also to be a kind of dead creature, from whom the living must flee and who is thus condemned to homelessness. Kafka was an amateur of etymology and very likely aware of the original sense of those haunting *"un-"* words, *"ungeheueres Ungeziefer"* ("monstrous vermin"), into which Gregor is transformed. *"Ungeheuer"* connotes the creature who has no place in the family; *"Ungeziefer,"* the unclean animal unsuited for sacrifice, the creature without a place in God's order.

Hence, the apparent realism with which Kafka describes the vermin should not conjure for the reader an insect of some definite kind. This would be to experience the vermin the way the cleaning woman does, who calls him "old dung beetle!" But "to forms of address like these Gregor would not respond"; they do not reflect his uncanny identity, which cannot be grasped in an image. A creature who could require the help of two strong persons to swing him out of bed cannot stick to the ceiling, however potent his glue. What sort of bug could watch, step by step, the approach of a man from behind him? True, at times Gregor may act like a beetle; but for one moment, when he is lured into the living room by his sister's violin playing, he is a pure spirit. Sometimes he behaves like a low sort of human being, a "louse"; but at other times he is an airy, flighty kind of creature. In the end he is sheerly not-this, not-that—a paradox, a creature not even of dust. He is a sign of that unnatural being in Kafka—the writer.

This equation is important because through it Kafka affirms his existence as a writer. Unlike *The Judgment,* this story does not propose that the father is in league with the vermin or that the vermin is his creature. The

---

* *Briefe 1902–1924,* ed. Max Brod (New York: Schocken Books, 1958), pp. 384–85.

origin of the metamorphosis remains radical, unnatural, and mysterious; the response of the father is to disclaim all connection with it. Psychoanalysis might prove that through this disaster he is secretly avenged on his son; but by this logic, too, the son is secretly avenged by his father's humiliation. The father is not the source of this bizarre and precarious existence; or Kafka would not have shown so clearly that Gregor is actually and independently of him a vermin. Yet this is what happens when the perspective shifts, just after Gregor's death, to authoritative omniscience, and we confront a dried up, inhuman corpse.

Gregor *is* this vermin; his metamorphosis "was no dream." Except for one moment of eagerness to see "today's fantasy . . . gradually fade away," he does not even express the desire to turn back into his original form. With some cause: his metamorphosis is not entirely a degradation, for it makes possible his first experience of music; before the metamorphosis, Gregor did not love music. Of course Gregor is deceived when he supposes that music will open a way for him toward the unknown nourishment he longs for. His pursuit of the music collapses into a pursuit of his sister and then into a death sentence. But even this moment seems less a sign of Gregor's vileness than of the writer's knowledge that the path of longing leads only to other longings. Gregor's experience of music has the very outcome that it does for the hero of *Amerika*, who feels "rising within him a sorrow which reached past the end of this song, seeking another end which it could not find." * "Art for the artist," said Kafka, "is only suffering through which he releases himself for further suffering." †

The Metamorphosis conveys Kafka's essential vision: to be a writer is to be condemned to irreparable estrangement. In writing about a monstrous non-being, Kafka

---

* *Amerika*, trans. Edwin Muir (New York: New Directions, 1946), p. 90. Muir incorrectly reads "Leid" (sorrow) as "Lied" (song).

† Gustav Janouch, *Conversations with Kafka*, trans. Goronwy Rees (New York: New Directions, 1969), p. 28.

writes about himself; but in doing so he also stays a little bit ahead of himself, for he is above all the narrator of the story, who survives the death of the vermin. Kafka's strength to contemplate his own death and survive it prepares him only for new deaths; yet in these deaths and survivals there is an element of play. About such scenes in his work Kafka wrote in 1914: "But for me, who believe that I shall be able to lie contentedly on my deathbed, such scenes are secretly a game." *

But the struggle to maintain the clarity of the writer is not always successful: Kafka frequently despairs. A later formulation reads: "What I have played at will really happen. I have not ransomed myself by writing. All my life I have been dead, and now I shall really die. My life was sweeter than others', my death will be that much more terrible. The writer in me of course will die at once, for such a figure has no basis, has no substance, isn't even of dust; it is only a little bit possible in the maddest earthly life, it is only a construction of the craving for enjoyment. This is the writer." †

It is unlikely that many of Kafka's readers since the war have been able to detect the playful element in any of his death scenes. His forecast of a terrible death for not having lived seems to express more exactly the mode, which seems to be the only mode, in which we now understand estrangement and whose extreme form is political terror. Unlike the artist, no political victim can wish to maintain his condition. As political estrangement becomes more and more the norm of Western society, and as capitalism, as Kafka said, becomes "the condition of the world and the soul," ‡ Kafka's late fears will more and more provide the frame in which we read his work. Nonetheless we will misunderstand him if we do not grasp that the way in which he experienced estrangement was literature, with an intensity greater than that of any other

---

* *Diaries, 1914–1923*, p. 102.

† *Briefe*, p. 385.

‡ Gustav Janouch, *Gespräche mit Kafka* (Frankfurt am Main: S. Fischer, 1968), p. 206.

writer of this century, more inexorably than Joyce or Proust or Mann. From this experience flows the power of Kafka's work to comprehend all forms of alienation, and to suggest a response to political estrangement different from political counterterror: the effort to illuminate this condition by grasping through literature that play is the reward for the courage of accepting death.

THE METAMORPHOSIS

I

When Gregor Samsa woke up one morning from unsettling dreams, he found himself changed in his bed into a monstrous vermin. He was lying on his back as hard as armor plate, and when he lifted his head a little, he saw his vaulted brown belly, sectioned by arch-shaped ribs, to whose dome the cover, about to slide off completely, could barely cling. His many legs, pitifully thin compared with the size of the rest of him, were waving helplessly before his eyes.

"What's happened to me?" he thought. It was no dream. His room. a regular human room, only a little on the small side lay quiet between the four familiar walls. Over the table, on which an unpacked line of fabric samples was all spread out—Samsa was a traveling salesman—hung the picture which he had recently cut out of a glossy magazine and lodged in a pretty gilt frame. It showed a lady done up in a fur hat and a fur boa, sitting upright and raising up against the viewer a heavy fur muff in which her whole forearm had disappeared.

Gregor's eyes then turned to the window, and the overcast weather—he could hear raindrops hitting against the metal window ledge—completely depressed him. "How about going back to sleep for a few minutes and forgetting all this nonsense," he thought, but that was completely impracticable, since he was used to sleeping on his right side and in his present state could not get into that position. No matter how hard he threw himself onto his right side. he always rocked onto his back again. He must have tried it a hundred times, closing his eyes so as not to have to see his squirming legs, and stopped only when he began to feel a slight, dull pain in his side, which he had never felt before.

3

"Oh God," he thought, "what a grueling job I've picked! Day in, day out—on the road. The upset of doing business is much worse than the actual business in the home office, and, besides, I've got the torture of traveling, worrying about changing trains, eating miserable food at all hours, constantly seeing new faces, no relationships that last or get more intimate. To the devil with it all!" He felt a slight itching up on top of his belly; shoved himself slowly on his back closer to the bedpost, so as to be able to lift his head better; found the itchy spot, studded with small white dots which he had no idea what to make of; and wanted to touch the spot with one of his legs but immediately pulled it back, for the contact sent a cold shiver through him.

He slid back again into his original position. "This getting up so early," he thought, "makes anyone a complete idiot. Human beings have to have their sleep. Other traveling salesmen live like harem women. For instance, when I go back to the hotel before lunch to write up the business I've done, these gentlemen are just having breakfast. That's all I'd have to try with my boss; I'd be fired on the spot. Anyway, who knows if that wouldn't be a very good thing for me. If I didn't hold back for my parents' sake, I would have quit long ago, I would have marched up to the boss and spoken my piece from the bottom of my heart. He would have fallen off the desk! It is funny, too, the way he sits on the desk and talks down from the heights to the employees, especially when they have to come right up close on account of the boss's being hard of hearing. Well, I haven't given up hope completely; once I've gotten the money together to pay off my parents' debt to him—that will probably take another five or six years—I'm going to do it without fail. Then I'm going to make the big break. But for the time being I'd better get up, since my train leaves at five."

And he looked over at the alarm clock, which was ticking on the chest of drawers. "God Almighty!" he thought. It was six-thirty, the hands were quietly moving forward, it was actually past the half-hour, it was already nearly a quarter to. Could it be that the alarm hadn't gone off?

You could see from the bed that it was set correctly for four o'clock; it certainly had gone off, too. Yes, but was it possible to sleep quietly through a ringing that made the furniture shake? Well, he certainly hadn't slept quietly, but probably all the more soundly for that. But what should he do now? The next train left at seven o'clock; to make it, he would have to hurry like a madman, and the line of samples wasn't packed yet, and he himself didn't feel especially fresh and ready to march around. And even if he did make the train, he could not avoid getting it from the boss, because the messenger boy had been waiting at the five-o'clock train and would have long ago reported his not showing up. He was a tool of the boss, without brains or backbone. What if he were to say he was sick? But that would be extremely embarrassing and suspicious because during his five years with the firm Gregor had not been sick even once. The boss would be sure to come with the health-insurance doctor, blame his parents for their lazy son, and cut off all excuses by quoting the health-insurance doctor, for whom the world consisted of people who were completely healthy but afraid to work. And, besides, in this case would he be so very wrong? In fact, Gregor felt fine, with the exception of his drowsiness, which was really unnecessary after sleeping so late, and he even had a ravenous appetite.

Just as he was thinking all this over at top speed, without being able to decide to get out of bed—the alarm clock had just struck a quarter to seven—he heard a cautious knocking at the door next to the head of his bed. "Gregor," someone called—it was his mother—"it's a quarter to seven. Didn't you want to catch the train?" What a soft voice! Gregor was shocked to hear his own voice answering, unmistakably his own voice, true, but in which, as if from below, an insistent distressed chirping intruded, which left the clarity of his words intact only for a moment really, before so badly garbling them as they carried that no one could be sure if he had heard right. Gregor had wanted to answer in detail and to explain everything, but, given the circumstances, confined himself to saying, "Yes, yes, thanks, Mother, I'm just getting up." The wooden door must have prevented the change in Gregor's voice from being noticed outside, because his mother was satisfied with this explanation and shuffled off. But their little exchange had made the rest of the family aware that, contrary to expectations, Gregor was still in the house, and already his father was knocking on one of the side doors, feebly but with his fist. "Gregor, Gregor," he called, "what's going on?" And after a little while he called again in a deeper, warning voice, "Gregor! Gregor!" At the other side door, however, his sister moaned gently, "Gregor? Is something the matter with you? Do you want anything?" Toward both sides Gregor answered: "I'm all ready," and made an effort, by meticulous pronunciation and by inserting long pauses between individual words, to eliminate everything from his voice that might betray him. His father went back to his breakfast, but his sister whispered, "Gregor, open up, I'm pleading with you." But Gregor had absolutely no intention of opening the door and complimented himself instead on the precaution he had adopted from his business trips, of locking all the doors during the night even at home.

First of all he wanted to get up quietly, without any excitement; get dressed; and, the main thing, have breakfast, and only then think about what to do next, for he saw clearly that in bed he would never think things through to a rational conclusion. He remembered how even in the past he had often felt some kind of slight pain, possibly caused by lying in an uncomfortable position, which, when he got up, turned out to be purely imaginary, and he was eager to see how today's fantasy would gradually fade away. That the change in his voice was nothing more than the first sign of a bad cold, an occupational ailment of the traveling salesman, he had no doubt in the least.

It was very easy to throw off the cover; all he had to do was puff himself up a little, and it fell off by itself. But after this, things got difficult, especially since he was so unusually broad. He would have needed hands and arms to lift himself up, but instead of that he had only his numerous little legs, which were in every different kind of perpetual motion and which, besides, he could not control. If he wanted to bend one, the first thing that happened was that it stretched itself out; * and if he finally succeeded in getting this leg to do what he wanted, all the others in the meantime, as if set free, began to work in the most intensely painful agitation. "Just don't stay in bed being useless," Gregor said to himself.

First he tried to get out of bed with the lower part of his body, but this lower part—which by the way he had not seen yet and which he could not form a clear picture of—proved too difficult to budge; it was taking so long; and when finally, almost out of his mind, he lunged forward with all his force, without caring, he had picked the wrong direction and slammed himself violently against the lower bedpost, and the searing pain he felt taught him that exactly the lower part of his body was, for the moment anyway, the most sensitive.

He therefore tried to get the upper part of his body out of bed first and warily turned his head toward the edge of the bed. This worked easily, and in spite of its width and weight the mass of his body finally followed, slowly, the movement of his head. But when at last he stuck his head over the edge of the bed into the air, he got too scared to continue any further, since if he finally let himself fall in this position, it would be a miracle if he didn't injure his head. And just now he had better not for the life of him lose consciousness; he would rather stay in bed.

But when, once again, after the same exertion, he lay in his original position, sighing, and again watched his little legs struggling, if possible more fiercely, with each other and saw no way of bringing peace and order into this mindless motion, he again told himself that it was impossible for him to stay in bed and that the most rational thing was to make any sacrifice for even the smallest hope of freeing himself from the bed. But at the same time he did not forget to remind himself occasionally that thinking

---

* he stretched himself out;

things over calmly—indeed, as calmly as possible—was much better than jumping to desperate decisions. At such moments he fixed his eyes as sharply as possible on the window, but unfortunately there was little confidence and cheer to be gotten from the view of the morning fog, which shrouded even the other side of the narrow street. "Seven o'clock already," he said to himself as the alarm clock struck again, "seven o'clock already and still such a fog." And for a little while he lay quietly, breathing shallowly, as if expecting, perhaps, from the complete silence the return of things to the way they really and naturally were.

But then he said to himself, "Before it strikes a quarter past seven, I must be completely out of bed without fail. Anyway, by that time someone from the firm will be here to find out where I am, since the office opens before seven." And now he started rocking the complete length of his body out of the bed with a smooth rhythm. If he let himself topple out of bed in this way, his head, which on falling he planned to lift up sharply, would presumably remain unharmed. His back seemed to be hard; nothing was likely to happen to it when it fell onto the carpet. His biggest misgiving came from his concern about the loud crash that was bound to occur and would probably create, if not terror, at least anxiety behind all the doors. But that would have to be risked.

When Gregor's body already projected halfway out of bed—the new method was more of a game than a struggle, he only had to keep on rocking and jerking himself along—he thought how simple everything would be if he could get some help. Two strong persons—he thought of his father and the maid—would have been completely sufficient; they would only have had to shove their arms under his arched back, in this way scoop him off the bed, bend down with their burden, and then just be careful and patient while he managed to swing himself down onto the floor, where his little legs would hopefully acquire some purpose. Well, leaving out the fact that the doors were locked, should he really call for help? In spite of all his miseries, he could not repress a smile at this thought.

He was already so far along that when he rocked more strongly he could hardly keep his balance, and very soon he would have to commit himself, because in five minutes it would be a quarter past seven—when the doorbell rang. "It's someone from the firm," he said to himself and almost froze, while his little legs only danced more quickly. For a moment everything remained quiet. "They're not going to answer," Gregor said to himself, captivated by some senseless hope. But then, of course, the maid went to the door as usual with her firm stride and opened up. Gregor only had to hear the visitor's first word of greeting to know who it was—the office manager himself. Why was only Gregor condemned to work for a firm where at the slightest omission they immediately suspected the worst? Were all employees louts without exception, wasn't there a single loyal, dedicated worker among them who, when he had not fully utilized a few hours of the morning for the firm, was driven half-mad by pangs of conscience and was actually unable to get out of bed? Really, wouldn't it have been enough to send one of the apprentices to find out—if this prying were absolutely necessary —did the manager himself have to come, and did the whole innocent family have to be shown in this way that the investigation of this suspicious affair could be entrusted only to the intellect of the manager? And more as a result of the excitement produced in Gregor by these thoughts than as a result of any real decision, he swung himself out of bed with all his might. There was a loud thump, but it was not a real crash. The fall was broken a little by the carpet, and Gregor's back was more elastic than he had thought, which explained the not very noticeable muffled sound. Only he had not held his head carefully enough and hit it; he turned it and rubbed it on the carpet in anger and pain.

"Something fell in there," said the manager in the room on the left. Gregor tried to imagine whether something like what had happened to him today could one day happen even to the manager; you really had to grant the possibility. But, as if in rude reply to this question, the manager took a few decisive steps in the next room and made his patent leather boots creak. From the room on the right his sister whispered, to inform Gregor, "Gregor, the manager is here." "I know," Gregor said to himself; but he did not dare raise his voice enough for his sister to hear.

"Gregor," his father now said from the room on the left, "the manager has come and wants to be informed why you didn't catch the early train. We don't know what we should say to him. Besides, he wants to speak to you personally. So please open the door. He will certainly be so kind as to excuse the disorder of the room." "Good morning, Mr. Samsa," the manager called in a friendly voice. "There's something the matter with him," his mother said to the manager while his father was still at the door, talking. "Believe me, sir, there's something the matter with him. Otherwise how would Gregor have missed a train? That boy has nothing on his mind but the business. It's almost begun to rile me that he never goes out nights. He's been back in the city for eight days now, but every night he's been home. He sits there with us at the table, quietly reading the paper or studying timetables. It's already a distraction for him when he's busy working with his fretsaw. For instance, in the span of two or three evenings he carved a little frame. You'll be amazed how pretty it is; it's hanging inside his room. You'll see it right away when Gregor opens the door. You know, I'm glad that you've come, sir. We would never have gotten Gregor to open the door by ourselves; he's so stubborn. And there's certainly something wrong with him, even though he said this morning there wasn't." "I'm coming right away," said Gregor slowly and deliberately, not moving in order not to miss a word of the conversation. "I haven't any other explanation myself," said the manager. "I hope it's nothing serious. On the other hand, I must say that we businessmen—fortunately or unfortunately, whichever you prefer—very often simply have to overcome a slight indisposition for business reasons." "So can the manager come in now?" asked his father, impatient, and knocked on the door again. "No," said Gregor. In the room on the left there was an embarrassing silence; in the room on the right his sister began to sob.

Why didn't his sister go in to the others? She had probably just got out of bed and not even started to get dressed. Then what was she crying about? Because he didn't get up and didn't let the manager in, because he was in danger of losing his job, and because then the boss would start hounding his parents about the old debts? For the time being, certainly, her worries were unnecessary. Gregor was still here and hadn't the slightest intention of letting the family down. True, at the moment he was lying on the carpet, and no one knowing his condition could seriously have expected him to let the manager in. But just because of this slight discourtesy, for which an appropriate excuse would easily be found later on, Gregor could not simply be dismissed. And to Gregor it seemed much more sensible to leave him alone now than to bother him with crying and persuasion. But it was just the uncertainty that was tormenting the others and excused their behavior.

"Mr. Samsa," the manager now called, raising his voice, "what's the matter? You barricade yourself in your room, answer only 'yes' and 'no,' cause your parents serious, unnecessary worry, and you neglect—I mention this only in passing—your duties to the firm in a really shocking manner. I am speaking here in the name of your parents and of your employer and ask you in all seriousness for an immediate, clear explanation. I'm amazed, amazed. I thought I knew you to be a quiet, reasonable person, and now you suddenly seem to want to start strutting about, flaunting strange whims. The head of the firm did suggest to me this morning a possible explanation for your tardiness—it concerned the cash payments recently entrusted to you—but really, I practically gave my word of honor that this explanation could not be right. But now, seeing your incomprehensible obstinacy, I am about to lose even the slightest desire to stick up for you in any way at all. And your job is not the most secure. Originally

I intended to tell you all this in private, but since you make me waste my time here for nothing, I don't see why your parents shouldn't hear too. Your performance of late has been very unsatisfactory; I know it is not the best season for doing business, we all recognize that; but a season for not doing any business, there is no such thing, Mr. Samsa. such a thing cannot be tolerated."

"But sir," cried Gregor, beside himself, in his excitement forgetting everything else, "I'm just opening up, in a minute. A slight indisposition, a dizzy spell, prevented me from getting up. I'm still in bed. But I already feel fine again. I'm just getting out of bed. Just be patient for a minute! I'm not as well as I thought yet. But really I'm fine. How something like this could just take a person by surprise! Only last night I was fine, my parents can tell you, or wait, last night I already had a slight premonition. They must have been able to tell by looking at me. Why didn't I report it to the office! But you always think that you'll get over a sickness without staying home. Sir! Spare my parents! There's no basis for any of the accusations that you're making against me now; no one has ever said a word to me about them. Perhaps you haven't seen the last orders I sent in. Anyway, I'm still going on the road with the eight o'clock train; these few hours of rest have done me good. Don't let me keep you, sir. I'll be at the office myself right away, and be so kind as to tell them this, and give my respects to the head of the firm."

And while Gregor hastily blurted all this out, hardly knowing what he was saying, he had easily approached the chest of drawers, probably as a result of the practice he had already gotten in bed, and now he tried to raise himself up against it. He actually intended to open the door, actually present himself and speak to the manager; he was eager to find out what the others, who were now so anxious to see him, would say at the sight of him. If they were shocked, then Gregor had no further responsibility and could be calm. But if they took everything calmly, then he, too, had no reason to get excited and could, if he hurried, actually be at the station by eight o'clock. At first he slid off the polished chest of drawers a few times, but at last, giving himself a final push, he stood upright; he no longer paid any attention to the pains in his abdomen, no matter how much they were burning. Now he let himself fall against the back of a nearby chair, clinging to its slats with his little legs. But by doing this he had gotten control of himself and fell silent, since he could now listen to what the manager was saying.

"Did you understand a word?" the manager was asking his parents. "He isn't trying to make fools of us, is he?" "My God," cried his mother, already in tears, "maybe he's seriously ill, and here we are, torturing him. Gretel Gretel!" she then cried. "Mother?" called his sister from the other side. They communicated by way of Gregor's room. "Go to the doctor's immediately. Gregor is sick. Hurry, get the doctor. Did you just hear Gregor talking?" "That was the voice of an animal," said the manager, in a tone conspicuously soft compared with the mother's yelling. "Anna!" "Anna!" the father called through the foyer into the kitchen, clapping his hands, "get a locksmith right away!" And already the two girls were running with rustling skirts through the foyer—how could his sister have gotten dressed so quickly?—and tearing open the door to the apartment. The door could not be heard slamming; they had probably left it open, as is the custom in homes where a great misfortune has occurred.

But Gregor had become much calmer. It was true that they no longer understood his words, though they had seemed clear enough to him, clearer than before, probably because his ear had grown accustomed to them. But still, the others now believed that there was something the matter with him and were ready to help him. The assurance and confidence with which the first measures had been taken did him good. He felt integrated into human society once again and hoped for marvelous, amazing feats from both the doctor and the locksmith, without really distinguishing sharply between them. In order to make his voice as clear as possible for the crucial discussions that were approaching, he cleared his throat a little —taking pains, of course, to do so in a very muffled manner, since this noise, too, might sound different from human coughing, a thing he no longer trusted himself to decide. In the next room, meanwhile, everything had become completely still. Perhaps his parents were sitting at the table with the manager, whispering; perhaps they were all leaning against the door and listening.

Gregor slowly lugged himself toward the door, pushing the chair in front of him, then let go of it, threw himself against the door, held himself upright against it—the pads on the bottom of his little legs exuded a little sticky substance—and for a moment rested there from the exertion. But then he got started turning the key in the lock with his mouth. Unfortunately it seemed that he had no real teeth—what was he supposed to grip the key with? —but in compensation his jaws, of course, were very strong; with their help he actually got the key moving and paid no attention to the fact that he was undoubtedly hurting himself in some way, for a brown liquid came out of his mouth, flowed over the key, and dripped onto the floor. "Listen," said the manager in the next room, "he's turning the key." This was great encouragement to Gregor; but everyone should have cheered him on, his father and mother too. "Go, Gregor," they should have called. "keep going, at that lock, harder, harder!" And in the delusion that they were all following his efforts with suspense, he clamped his jaws madly on the key with all the strength he could muster. Depending on the progress of the key, he danced around the lock; holding himself upright only by his mouth, he clung to the key, as the situation demanded, or pressed it down again with the whole weight of his body. The clearer click of the lock as it finally snapped back literally woke Gregor up. With a sigh of relief he said to himself, "So I didn't need the locksmith after all," and laid his head down on the handle in order to open wide [one wing of the double doors.] *

Since he had to use this method of opening the door, it was really opened very wide while he himself was still invisible. He first had to edge slowly around the one wing of the door, and do so very carefully if he was not to

---

* Literally, "the door." [S.C.]

fall flat on his back just before entering. He was still busy with this difficult maneuver and had no time to pay attention to anything else when he heard the manager burst out with a loud "Oh!"—it sounded like a rush of wind—and now he could see him, standing closest to the door, his hand pressed over his open mouth, slowly backing away, as if repulsed by an invisible, unrelenting force. His mother—in spite of the manager's presence she stood with her hair still unbraided from the night, sticking out in all directions—first looked at his father with her hands clasped, then took two steps toward Gregor, and sank down in the midst of her skirts spreading out around her, her face completely hidden on her breast. With a hostile expression his father clenched his fist, as if to drive Gregor back into his room, then looked uncertainly around the living room, shielded his eyes with his hands, and sobbed with heaves of his powerful chest.

Now Gregor did not enter the room after all but leaned against the inside of the firmly bolted wing of the door, so that only half his body was visible and his head above it, cocked to one side and peeping out at the others. In the meantime it had grown much lighter; across the street one could see clearly a section of the endless, grayish-black building opposite—it was a hospital—with its regular windows starkly piercing the façade; the rain was still coming down, but only in large, separately visible drops that were also pelting the ground literally one at a time. The breakfast dishes were laid out lavishly on the table, since for his father breakfast was the most important meal of the day, which he would prolong for hours while reading various newspapers. On the wall directly opposite hung a photograph of Gregor from his army days, in a lieutenant's uniform, his hand on his sword, a carefree smile on his lips, demanding respect for his bearing and his rank. The door to the foyer was open, and since the front door was open too, it was possible to see out onto the landing and the top of the stairs going down.

"Well," said Gregor—and he was thoroughly aware of being the only one who had kept calm—"I'll get dressed right away, pack up my samples, and go. Will you, will

you please let me go? Now, sir, you see, I'm not stubborn and I'm willing to work; traveling is a hardship, but
without it I couldn't live. Where are you going, sir? To
the office? Yes? Will you give an honest report of everything? A man might find for a moment that he was unable to work, but that's exactly the right time to remember
his past accomplishments and to consider that later on,
when the obstacle has been removed, he's bound to work
all the harder and more efficiently. I'm under so many
obligations to the head of the firm, as you know very well.
Besides, I also have my parents and my sister to worry
about. I'm in a tight spot, but I'll also work my way out
again. Don't make things harder for me than they already
are. Stick up for me in the office, please. Traveling salesmen aren't well liked there, I know. People think they
make a fortune leading the gay life. No one has any particular reason to rectify this prejudice. But you, sir, you
have a better perspective on things than the rest of the
office, an even better perspective, just between the two
of us, than the head of the firm himself, who in his capacity as owner easily lets his judgment be swayed against
an employee. And you also know very well that the traveling salesman, who is out of the office practically the whole
year round, can so easily become the victim of gossip,
coincidences, and unfounded accusations, against which
he's completely unable to defend himself, since in most
cases he knows nothing at all about them except when
he returns exhausted from a trip, and back home gets to
suffer on his own person the grim consequences, which
can no longer be traced back to their causes. Sir, don't
go away without a word to tell me you think I'm at least
partly right!"

But at Gregor's first words the manager had already
turned away and with curled lips looked back at Gregor
only over his twitching shoulder. And during Gregor's
speech he did not stand still for a minute but, without
letting Gregor out of his sight, backed toward the door,
yet very gradually, as if there were some secret prohibi-
tion against leaving the room. He was already in the
foyer, and from the sudden movement with which he

took his last step from the living room, one might have thought he had just burned the sole of his foot. In the foyer, however, he stretched his right hand far out toward the staircase, as if nothing less than an unearthly deliverance were awaiting him there.

Gregor realized that he must on no account let the manager go away in this mood if his position in the firm were not to be jeopardized in the extreme. His parents did not understand this too well; in the course of the years they had formed the conviction that Gregor was set for life in this firm; and furthermore, they were so preoccupied with their immediate troubles that they had lost all consideration for the future. But Gregor had this forethought. The manager must be detained, calmed down, convinced, and finally won over; Gregor's and the family's future depended on it! If only his sister had been there! She was perceptive; she had already begun to cry when Gregor was still lying calmly on his back. And certainly the manager, this ladies' man, would have listened to her; she would have shut the front door and in the foyer talked him out of his scare. But his sister was not there, Gregor had to handle the situation himself. And without stopping to realize that he had no idea what his new faculties of movement were, and without stopping to realize either that his speech had possibly —indeed, probably—not been understood again, he let go of the wing of the door; he shoved himself through the opening, intending to go to the manager, who was already on the landing, ridiculously holding onto the banisters with both hands; but groping for support, Gregor immediately fell down with a little cry onto his numerous little legs. This had hardly happened when for the first time that morning he had a feeling of physical well-being; his little legs were on firm ground; they obeyed him completely, as he noted to his joy; they even strained to carry him away wherever he wanted to go; and he already believed that final recovery from all his sufferings was imminent. But at that very moment, as he lay on the floor rocking with repressed motion, not far from his mother and just opposite her, she, who had seemed so completely self-absorbed, all at once jumped up, her arms stretched wide, her fingers spread, and cried, "Help, for God's sake, help!" held her head bent as if to see Gregor better, but inconsistently darted madly backward instead; had forgotten that the table laden with the breakfast dishes stood behind her; sat down on it hastily, as if her thoughts were elsewhere, when she reached it; and did not seem to notice at all that near her the big coffeepot had been knocked over and coffee was pouring in a steady stream onto the rug.

"Mother, Mother," said Gregor softly and looked up at her. For a minute the manager had completely slipped his mind; on the other hand at the sight of the spilling coffee he could not resist snapping his jaws several times in the air. At this his mother screamed once more, fled from the table, and fell into the arms of his father, who came rushing up to her. But Gregor had no time now for his parents; the manager was already on the stairs; with his chin on the banister, he was taking a last look back. Gregor was off to a running start, to be as sure as possible of catching up with him; the manager must have suspected something like this, for he leaped down several steps and disappeared; but still he shouted "Agh," and the sound carried through the whole staircase. Unfortunately the manager's flight now seemed to confuse his father completely, who had been relatively calm until now, for instead of running after the manager himself, or at least not hindering Gregor in his pursuit, he seized in his right hand the manager's cane, which had been left behind on a chair with his hat and overcoat, picked up in his left hand a heavy newspaper from the table, and stamping his feet, started brandishing the cane and the newspaper to drive Gregor back into his room. No plea of Gregor's helped, no plea was even understood; however humbly he might turn his head, his father merely stamped his feet more forcefully. Across the room his mother had thrown open a window in spite of the cool weather, and leaning out, she buried her face, far outside the window, in her hands. Between the alley and the staircase a strong draft was created, the window curtains blew in, the newspapers on the table rustled, single sheets fluttered across the floor. Pitilessly his father came on, hissing like a wild man. Now Gregor had not had any practice at all walking in reverse, it was really very slow going. If Gregor had only been allowed to turn around, he could have gotten into his room right away, but he was afraid to make his father impatient by this time-consuming gyration, and at any minute the cane in his father's hand threatened to come down on his back or his head with a deadly blow. Finally, however, Gregor had no choice, for he noticed with horror that in reverse he could not even keep going in one direction; and so, incessantly throwing uneasy side-glances at his father, he began to turn around as quickly as possible, in reality turning only very slowly. Perhaps his father realized his good intentions, for he did not interfere with him; instead, he even now and then directed the maneuver from afar with the tip of his cane. If only his father did not keep making this intolerable hissing sound! It made Gregor lose his head completely. He had almost finished the turn when—his mind continually on this hissing—he made a mistake and even started turning back around to his original position. But when he had at last successfully managed to get his head in front of the opened door, it turned out that his body was too broad to get through as it was. Of course in his father's present state of mind it did not even remotely occur to him to open the other wing of the door in order to give Gregor enough room to pass through. He had only the fixed idea that Gregor must return to his room as quickly as possible. He would never have allowed the complicated preliminaries Gregor needed to go through in order to stand up on one end and perhaps in this way fit through the door. Instead * he drove Gregor on, as if there were no obstacle, with exceptional loudness; the voice behind Gregor did not sound like that of only a single father; now this was really no joke any more, and Gregor forced himself—come what may—into the doorway. One side of his body rose up, he lay lop-sided in the opening, one of his flanks was scraped raw, ugly blotches

---

* Perhaps

marred the white door, soon he got stuck and could not
have budged any more by himself, his little legs on one
side dangled tremblingly in midair, those on the other
were painfully crushed against the floor—when from behind his father gave him a hard shove, which was truly
his salvation, and bleeding profusely, he flew far into his
room. The door was slammed shut with the cane, then
at last everything was quiet.

II

It was already dusk when Gregor awoke from his deep, comalike sleep. Even if he had not been disturbed, he would certainly not have woken up much later, for he felt that he had rested and slept long enough, but it seemed to him that a hurried step and a cautious shutting of the door leading to the foyer had awakened him. The light of the electric street-lamps * lay in pallid streaks on the ceiling and on the upper parts of the furniture, but underneath, where Gregor was, it was dark. Groping clumsily with his antennae, which he was only now † beginning to appreciate, he slowly dragged himself toward the door to see what had been happening there. His left side felt like one single long, unpleasantly tautening scar, and he actually had to limp on his two rows of legs. Besides, one little leg had been seriously injured in the course of the morning's events—it was almost a miracle that only one had been injured—and dragged along lifelessly.

Only after he got to the door did he notice what had really attracted him—the smell of something to eat. For there stood a bowl filled with fresh milk, in which small slices of white bread were floating. He could almost have laughed for joy, since he was even hungrier than he had been in the morning, and he immediately dipped his head into the milk, almost to over his eyes. But he soon drew it back again in disappointment; not only because he had difficulty eating on account of the soreness in his left side—and he could eat only if his whole panting body cooperated—but because he didn't like the milk at all, al-

* streetcar
† he was now first

21

though it used to be his favorite drink, and that was
certainly why his sister had put it in the room; in fact,
he turned away from the bowl almost with repulsion and
crawled back to the middle of the room.

In the living room, as Gregor saw through the crack in
the door, the gas had been lit, but while at this hour of
the day his father was in the habit of reading the afternoon newspaper in a loud voice to his mother and sometimes to his sister too, now there wasn't a sound. Well,
perhaps this custom of reading aloud, which his sister
was always telling him and writing him about, had recently been discontinued altogether. But in all the other
rooms too it was just as still, although the apartment certainly was not empty. "What a quiet life the family has
been leading," Gregor said to himself, and while he
stared rigidly in front of him into the darkness, he felt
very proud that he had been able to provide such a life
in so nice an apartment for his parents and his sister. But
what now if all the peace, the comfort, the contentment
were to come to a horrible end? In order not to get involved in such thoughts, Gregor decided to keep moving,
and he crawled up and down the room.

During the long evening first one of the side doors and
then the other was opened a small crack and quickly shut
again; someone had probably had the urge to come in
and then had had second thoughts. Gregor now settled
into position right by the living-room door, determined
somehow to get the hesitating visitor to come in, or at
least to find out who it might be; but the door was not
opened again, and Gregor waited in vain. In the morning,
when the doors had been locked, everyone had wanted to
come in; now that he had opened one of the doors and
the others had evidently been opened during the day, no
one came in, and now the keys were even inserted on
the outside.

It was late at night when the light finally went out in
the living room, and now it was easy for Gregor to tell
that his parents and his sister had stayed up so long,
since, as he could distinctly hear, all three were now
retiring on tiptoe. Certainly no one would come in to

Gregor until the morning; and so he had ample time to consider undisturbed how best to rearrange his life. But the empty high-ceilinged room in which he was forced to lie flat on the floor made him nervous, without his being able to tell why—since it was, after all, the room in which he had lived for the past five years—and turning half unconsciously and not without a slight feeling of shame, he scuttled under the couch where, although his back was a little crushed and he could not raise his head any more, he immediately felt very comfortable and was only sorry that his body was too wide to go completely under the couch.

There he stayed the whole night, which he spent partly in a sleepy trance, from which hunger pangs kept waking him with a start, partly in worries and vague hopes, all of which, however, led to the conclusion that for the time being he would have to lie low and, by being patient and showing his family every possible consideration, help them bear the inconvenience which he simply had to cause them in his present condition.

Early in the morning—it was still almost night—Gregor had the opportunity of testing the strength of the resolutions he had just made, for his sister, almost fully dressed, opened the door from the foyer and looked in eagerly. She did not see him right away, but when she caught sight of him under the couch—God, he had to be somewhere, he couldn't just fly away—she became so frightened that she lost control of herself and slammed the door shut again. But, as if she felt sorry for her behavior, she immediately opened the door again and came in on tiptoe, as if she were visiting someone seriously ill or perhaps even a stranger. Gregor had pushed his head forward just to the edge of the couch and was watching her. Would she notice that he had left the milk standing, and not because he hadn't been hungry, and would she bring in a dish of something he'd like better? If she were not going to do it of her own free will, he would rather starve than call it to her attention, although, really, he felt an enormous urge to shoot out from under the couch, throw himself at his sister's feet, and beg her for something good to eat. But his sister noticed at once, to her astonishment, that the bowl was still full, only a little milk was spilled around it; she picked it up immediately—not with her bare hands, of course, but with a rag—and carried it out. Gregor was extremely curious to know what she would bring him instead, and he racked his brains on the subject. But he would never have been able to guess what his sister, in the goodness of her heart, actually did. To find out his likes and dislikes, she brought him a wide assortment of things, all spread out on an old newspaper: old, half-rotten vegetables; bones left over from the evening meal, caked with congealed white sauce; some raisins and almonds; a piece of cheese, which two days before Gregor had declared inedible; a plain slice of bread, a slice of bread and butter, and one with butter and salt. In addition to all this she put down some water in the bowl apparently permanently earmarked for Gregor's use. And out of a sense of delicacy, since she knew that Gregor would not eat in front of her, she left hurriedly and even turned the key, just so that Gregor should know that he might make himself as comfortable as he wanted. Gregor's legs began whirring now that he was going to eat. Besides, his bruises must have completely healed, since he no longer felt any handicap, and marveling at this he thought how, over a month ago, he had cut his finger very slightly with a knife and how this wound was still hurting him only the day before yesterday. "Have I become less sensitive?" he thought, already sucking greedily at the cheese, which had immediately and forcibly attracted him ahead of all the other dishes. One right after the other, and with eyes streaming with tears of contentment, he devoured the cheese, the vegetables, and the sauce; the fresh foods, on the other hand, he did not care for; he couldn't even stand their smell and even dragged the things he wanted to eat a bit farther away. He had finished with everything long since and was just lying lazily at the same spot when his sister slowly turned the key as a sign for him to withdraw. That immediately startled him, although he was almost asleep, and he scuttled under the couch again. But it took great self-control for him to stay under the couch even for the short time his sister was in the room, since his body had become a little bloated from the heavy meal, and in his cramped position he could hardly breathe. In between slight attacks of suffocation he watched with bulging eyes as his unsuspecting sister took a broom and swept up, not only his leavings, but even the foods which Gregor had left completely untouched—as if they too were no longer usable—and dumping everything hastily into a pail, which she covered with a wooden lid, she carried everything out. She had hardly turned her back when Gregor came out from under the couch, stretching and puffing himself up.

This, then, was the way Gregor was fed each day, once in the morning, when his parents and the maid were still asleep, and a second time in the afternoon after everyone had had dinner, for then his parents took a short nap again, and the maid could be sent out by his sister on some errand. Certainly they did not want him to starve either, but perhaps they would not have been able to stand knowing any more about his meals than from hearsay, or perhaps his sister wanted to spare them even what was possibly only a minor torment, for really, they were suffering enough as it was.

Gregor could not find out what excuses had been made to get rid of the doctor and the locksmith on that first morning, for since the others could not understand what he said, it did not occur to any of them, not even to his sister, that he could understand what they said, and so he had to be satisfied, when his sister was in the room, with only occasionally hearing her sighs and appeals to the saints. It was only later, when she had begun to get used to everything—there could never, of course, be any question of a complete adjustment—that Gregor sometimes caught a remark which was meant to be friendly or could be interpreted as such. "Oh, he liked what he had today," she would say when Gregor had tucked away a good helping, and in the opposite case, which gradually occurred more and more frequently, she used to say, almost sadly, "He's left everything again."

But if Gregor could not get any news directly, he overheard a great deal from the neighboring rooms, and as soon as he heard voices, he would immediately run to the door concerned and press his whole body against it. Especially in the early days, there was no conversation that was not somehow about him, if only implicitly. For two whole days there were family consultations at every mealtime about how they should cope; this was also the topic of discussion between meals, for at least two members of the family were always at home, since no one probably wanted to stay home alone and it was impossible to leave the apartment completely empty. Besides, on the very first day the maid—it was not completely clear what and how much she knew of what had happened—had begged his mother on bended knees to dismiss her immediately; and when she said goodbye a quarter of an hour later, she thanked them in tears for the dismissal, as if for the greatest favor that had ever been done to her in this house, and made a solemn vow, without anyone asking her for it, not to give anything away to anyone.

Now his sister, working with her mother, had to do the cooking too; of course that did not cause her much trouble, since they hardly ate anything. Gregor was always hearing one of them pleading in vain with one of the others to eat and getting no answer except, "Thanks, I've had enough," or something similar. They did not seem to drink anything either. His sister often asked her father if he wanted any beer and gladly offered to go out for it herself; and when he did not answer, she said, in order to remove any hesitation on his part, that she could also send the janitor's wife to get it, but then his father finally answered with a definite "No," and that was the end of that.

In the course of the very first day his father explained the family's financial situation and prospects to both the mother and the sister. From time to time he got up from the table to get some kind of receipt or notebook out of the little strongbox he had rescued from the collapse of his business five years before. Gregor heard him open the complicated lock and secure it again after taking out what he had been looking for. These explanations by his

father were to some extent the first pleasant news Gregor
had heard since his imprisonment. He had always believed that his father had not been able to save a penny
from the business, at least his father had never told him
anything to the contrary, and Gregor, for his part, had
never asked him any questions. In those days Gregor's
sole concern had been to do everything in his power to
make the family forget as quickly as possible the business disaster which had plunged everyone into a state of
total despair. And so he had begun to work with special
ardor and had risen almost overnight from stock clerk to
traveling salesman, which of course had opened up very
different money-making possibilities, and in no time his
successes on the job were transformed, by means of com-
missions, into hard cash that could be plunked down on
the table at home in front of his astonished and delighted
family. Those had been wonderful times, and they had
never returned, at least not with the same glory, although
later on Gregor earned enough money to meet the ex-
penses of the entire family and actually did so They had
just gotten used to it, the family as well as Gregor, the
money was received with thanks and given with pleasure,
but no special feeling of warmth went with it any more.
Only his sister had remained close to Gregor, and it was
his secret plan that she who, unlike him, loved music and
could play the violin movingly, should be sent next year
to the Conservatory, regardless of the great expense involved, which could surely be made up for in some other
way. Often during Gregor's short stays in the city the
Conservatory would come up in his conversations with his
sister, but always merely as a beautiful dream which was
not supposed to come true, and his parents were not
happy to hear even these innocent allusions; but Gregor
had very concrete ideas on the subject and he intended
solemnly to announce his plan on Christmas Eve.

Thoughts like these, completely useless in his present
state, went through his head as he stood glued to the door,
listening. Sometimes out of general exhaustion he could
not listen any more and let his head bump carelessly
against the door, but immediately pulled it back again, for

even the slight noise he made by doing this had been
heard in the next room and made them all lapse into
silence. "What's he carrying on about in there now?" said
his father after a while, obviously turning toward the
door, and only then would the interrupted conversation
gradually be resumed.

Gregor now learned in a thorough way—for his father
was in the habit of often repeating himself in his explanations, partly because he himself had not dealt with these
matters for a long time, partly, too, because his mother
did not understand everything the first time around—that
in spite of all their misfortunes a bit of capital, a very
little bit, certainly, was still intact from the old days,
which in the meantime had increased a little through the
untouched interest. But besides that, the money Gregor
had brought home every month—he had kept only a few
dollars for himself—had never been completely used up
and had accumulated into a tidy principal. Behind his
door Gregor nodded emphatically, delighted at this unexpected foresight and thrift. Of course he actually could
have paid off more of his father's debt to the boss with
this extra money, and the day on which he could have
gotten rid of his job would have been much closer, but
now things were undoubtedly better the way his father
had arranged them.

Now this money was by no means enough to let the
family live off the interest; the principal was perhaps
enough to support the family for one year, or at the most
two, but that was all there was. So it was just a sum that
really should not be touched and that had to be put away
for a rainy day; but the money to live on would have to
be earned. Now his father was still healthy, certainly, but
he was an old man who had not worked for the past five
years and who in any case could not be expected to
undertake too much; during these five years, which were
the first vacation of his hard-working yet unsuccessful life,
he had gained a lot of weight and as a result had become
fairly sluggish. And was his old mother now supposed to
go out and earn money, when she suffered from asthma,
when a walk through the apartment was already an or-

deal for her, and when she spent every other day lying on the sofa under the open window, gasping for breath? And was his sister now supposed to work—who for all her seventeen years was still a child and whom it would be such a pity to deprive of the life she had led until now, which had consisted of wearing pretty clothes, sleeping late, helping in the house, enjoying a few modest amusements, and above all playing the violin? At first, whenever the conversation turned to the necessity of earning money, Gregor would let go of the door and throw himself down on the cool leather sofa which stood beside it, for he felt hot with shame and grief.

Ofter he lay there the whole long night through, not sleeping a wink and only scrabbling on the leather for hours on end. Or, not balking at the huge effort of pushing an armchair to the window, he would crawl up to the window sill and, propped up in the chair, lean against the window, evidently in some sort of remembrance of the feeling of freedom he used to have from looking out the window. For, in fact, from day to day he saw things even a short distance away less and less distinctly; the hospital opposite, which he used to curse because he saw so much of it, was now completely beyond his range of vision, and if he had not been positive that he was living in Charlotte Street—a quiet but still very much a city street—he might have believed that he was looking out of his window into a desert where the gray sky and the gray earth were indistinguishably fused. It took his observant sister only twice to notice that his armchair was standing by the window for her to push the chair back to the same place by the window each time she had finished cleaning the room, and from then on she even left the inside casement of the window open.

If Gregor had only been able to speak to his sister and thank her for everything she had to do for him, he could have accepted her services more easily; as it was, they caused him pain. Of course his sister tried to ease the embarrassment of the whole situation as much as possible, and as time went on, she naturally managed it better and better, but in time Gregor, too, saw things much more clearly. Even the way she came in was terrible for him. Hardly had she entered the room than she would run straight to the window without taking time to close the door—though she was usually so careful to spare everyone the sight of Gregor's room—then tear open the casements with eager hands, almost as if she were suffocating, and remain for a little while at the window even in the coldest weather, breathing deeply. With this racing and crashing she frightened Gregor twice a day; the whole time he cowered under the couch, and yet he knew very well that she would certainly have spared him this if only she had found it possible to stand being in a room with him with the window closed.

One time—it must have been a month since Gregor's metamorphosis, and there was certainly no particular reason any more for his sister to be astonished at Gregor's appearance—she came a little earlier than usual and caught Gregor still looking out the window, immobile and so in an excellent position to be terrifying. It would not have surprised Gregor if she had not come in, because his position prevented her from immediately opening the window, but not only did she not come in, she even sprang back and locked the door; a stranger might easily have thought that Gregor had been lying in wait for her, wanting to bite her. Of course Gregor immediately hid under the couch, but he had to wait until noon before his sister came again, and she seemed much more uneasy than usual. He realized from this that the sight of him was still repulsive to her and was bound to remain repulsive to her in the future, and that she probably had to overcome a lot of resistance not to run away at the sight of even the small part of his body that jutted out from under the couch. So, to spare her even this sight, one day he carried the sheet on his back to the couch—the job took four hours—and arranged it in such a way that he was now completely covered up and his sister could not see him even when she stooped. If she had considered this sheet unnecessary, then of course she could have removed it, for it was clear enough that it could not be for his own pleasure that Gregor shut himself off altogether, but she left the sheet the way it was, and Gregor thought that he had even caught a grateful look when one time he cautiously lifted the sheet a little with his head in order to see how his sister was taking the new arrangement.

During the first two weeks, his parents could not bring themselves to come in to him, and often he heard them say how much they appreciated his sister's work, whereas until now they had frequently been annoyed with her because she had struck them as being a little useless. But now both of them, his father and his mother, often waited outside Gregor's room while his sister straightened it up, and as soon as she came out she had to tell them in great detail how the room looked, what Gregor had eaten, how he had behaved this time, and whether he had perhaps shown a little improvement. His mother, incidentally, began relatively soon to want to visit Gregor, but his father and his sister at first held her back with reasonable arguments to which Gregor listened very attentively and of which he whole-heartedly approved. But later she had to be restrained by force, and then when she cried out, "Let me go to Gregor, he is my unfortunate boy! Don't you understand that I have to go to him?" Gregor thought that it might be a good idea after all if his mother did come in, not every day of course, but perhaps once a week; she could still do everything much better than his sister, who, for all her courage, was still only a child and in the final analysis had perhaps taken on such a difficult assignment only out of childish flightiness.

Gregor's desire to see his mother was soon fulfilled. During the day Gregor did not want to show himself at the window, if only out of consideration for his parents, but he couldn't crawl very far on his few square yards of floor space, either; he could hardly put up with just lying still even at night; eating soon stopped giving him the slightest pleasure, so, as a distraction, he adopted the habit of crawling crisscross over the walls and the ceiling. He especially liked hanging from the ceiling; it was completely different from lying on the floor; one could breathe

more freely; a faint swinging sensation went through the
body; and in the almost happy absent-mindedness which
Gregor felt up there, it could happen to his own surprise
that he let go and plopped onto the floor. But now, of
course, he had much better control of his body than
before and did not hurt himself even from such a big
drop. His sister immediately noticed the new entertain-
ment Gregor had discovered for himself—after all, he left
behind traces of his sticky substance wherever he crawled
—and so she got it into her head to make it possible for
Gregor to crawl on an altogether wider scale by taking
out the furniture which stood in his way—mainly the
chest of drawers and the desk. But she was not able to
do this by herself; she did not dare ask her father for
help; the maid would certainly not have helped her, for
although this girl, who was about sixteen, was bravely
sticking it out after the previous cook had left, she had
asked for the favor of locking herself in the kitchen at
all times and of only opening the door on special request.
So there was nothing left for his sister to do except to
get her mother one day when her father was out. And his
mother did come, with exclamations of excited joy, but
she grew silent at the door of Gregor's room. First his
sister looked to see, of course, that everything in the
room was in order; only then did she let her mother
come in. Hurrying as fast as he could, Gregor had pulled
the sheet down lower still and pleated it more tightly—
it really looked just like a sheet accidently thrown
over the couch. This time Gregor also refrained from
spying from under the sheet; he renounced seeing his
mother for the time being and was simply happy that she
had come after all. "Come on, you can't see him," his
sister said, evidently leading her mother in by the hand.
Now Gregor could hear the two frail women moving the
old chest of drawers—heavy for anyone—from its place
and his sister insisting on doing the harder part of the
job herself, ignoring the warnings of her mother, who was
afraid that she would overexert herself. It went on for
a long time. After struggling for a good quarter of an
hour, his mother said that they had better leave the

chest where it was, because, in the first place, it was too heavy, they would not finish before his father came, and with the chest in the middle of the room, Gregor would be completely barricaded; and, in the second place, it was not at all certain that they were doing Gregor a favor by removing his furniture. To her the opposite seemed to be the case; the sight of the bare wall was heartbreaking; and why shouldn't Gregor also have the same feeling, since he had been used to his furniture for so long and would feel abandoned in the empty room. "And doesn't it look," his mother concluded very softly—in fact she had been almost whispering the whole time, as if she wanted to avoid letting Gregor, whose exact whereabouts she did not know, hear even the sound of her voice, for she was convinced that he did not understand the words—"and doesn't it look as if by removing his furniture we were showing him that we have given up all hope of his getting better and are leaving him to his own devices without any consideration? I think the best thing would be to try to keep the room exactly the way it was before, so that when Gregor comes back to us again, he'll find everything unchanged and can forget all the more easily what's happened in the meantime."

When he heard his mother's words, Gregor realized that the monotony of family life, combined with the fact that not a soul had addressed a word directly to him, must have addled his brain in the course of the past two months, for he could not explain to himself in any other way how in all seriousness he could have been anxious to have his room cleared out. Had he really wanted to have his warm room, comfortably fitted with furniture that had always been in the family, changed into a cave, in which, of course, he would be able to crawl around unhampered in all directions but at the cost of simultaneously, rapidly, and totally forgetting his human past? Even now he had been on the verge of forgetting, and only his mother's voice, which he had not heard for so long, had shaken him up. Nothing should be removed; everything had to stay; he could not do without the beneficial influence of the furniture on his state of mind;

and if the furniture prevented him from carrying on this senseless crawling around, then that was no loss but rather a great advantage.

But his sister unfortunately had a different opinion; she had become accustomed, certainly not entirely without justification, to adopt with her parents the role of the particularly well-qualified expert whenever Gregor's affairs were being discussed; and so her mother's advice was now sufficient reason for her to insist, not only on the removal of the chest of drawers and the desk, which was all she had been planning at first, but also on the removal of all the furniture with the exception of the indispensable couch. Of course it was not only childish defiance and the self-confidence she had recently acquired so unexpectedly and at such a cost that led her to make this demand; she had in fact noticed that Gregor needed plenty of room to crawl around in; and on the other hand, as best she could tell, he never used the furniture at all. Perhaps, however, the romantic enthusiasm of girls her age, which seeks to indulge itself at every opportunity, played a part, by tempting her to make Gregor's situation even more terrifying in order that she might do even more for him. Into a room in which Gregor ruled the bare walls all alone, no human being beside Grete was ever likely to set foot.

And so she did not let herself be swerved from her decision by her mother, who, besides, from the sheer anxiety of being in Gregor's room, seemed unsure of herself, soon grew silent, and helped her daughter as best she could to get the chest of drawers out of the room. Well, in a pinch Gregor could do without the chest, but the desk had to stay. And hardly had the women left the room with the chest, squeezing against it and groaning, than Gregor stuck his head out from under the couch to see how he could feel his way into the situation as considerately as possible. But unfortunately it had to be his mother who came back first, while in the next room Grete was clasping the chest and rocking it back and forth by herself, without of course budging it from the spot. His mother, however, was not used to the sight of

Gregor, he could have made her ill, and so Gregor, frightened, scuttled in reverse to the far end of the couch but could not stop the sheet from shifting a little at the front. That was enough to put his mother on the alert. She stopped, stood still for a moment, and then went back to Grete.

Although Gregor told himself over and over again that nothing special was happening, only a few pieces of furniture were being moved, he soon had to admit that this coming and going of the women, their little calls to each other, the scraping of the furniture along the floor had the effect on him of a great turmoil swelling on all sides, and as much as he tucked in his head and his legs and shrank until his belly touched the floor, he was forced to admit that he would not be able to stand it much longer. They were clearing out his room; depriving him of everything that he loved; they had already carried away the chest of drawers, in which he kept the fretsaw and other tools; were now budging the desk firmly embedded in the floor, the desk he had done his homework on when he was a student at business college, in high school, yes, even in public school—now he really had no more time to examine the good intentions of the two women, whose existence, besides, he had almost forgotten, for they were so exhausted that they were working in silence, and one could hear only the heavy shuffling of their feet.

And so he broke out—the women were just leaning against the desk in the next room to catch their breath for a minute—changed his course four times, he really didn't know what to salvage first, then he saw hanging conspicuously on the wall, which was otherwise bare already. the picture of the lady all dressed in furs, hurriedly crawled up on it and pressed himself against the glass, which gave a good surface to stick to and soothed his hot belly. At least no one would take away this picture, while Gregor completely covered it up. He turned his head toward the living-room door to watch the women when they returned.

They had not given themselves much of a rest and

were already coming back; Grete had put her arm
around her mother and was practically carrying her. "So
what should we take now?" said Grete and looked
around. At that her eyes met Gregor's as he clung to the
wall. Probably only because of her mother's presence
she kept her self-control, bent her head down to her
mother to keep her from looking around, and said, though
in a quavering and thoughtless voice: "Come, we'd better
go back into the living room for a minute." Grete's intent
was clear to Gregor, she wanted to bring his mother into
safety and then chase him down from the wall. Well, just
let her try! He squatted on his picture and would not
give it up. He would rather fly in Grete's face.

But Grete's words had now made her mother really
anxious; she stepped to one side, caught sight of the
gigantic brown blotch on the flowered wallpaper, and
before it really dawned on her that what she saw was
Gregor, cried in a hoarse, bawling voice: "Oh, God,
Oh, God!"; and as if giving up completely, she fell with
outstretched arms across the couch and did not stir. "You,
Gregor!" cried his sister with raised fist and piercing eyes.
These were the first words she had addressed directly
to him since his metamorphosis. She ran into the next
room to get some kind of spirits to revive her mother;
Gregor wanted to help too—there was time to rescue the
picture—but he was stuck to the glass and had to tear
himself loose by force; then he too ran into the next
room, as if he could give his sister some sort of advice,
as in the old days; but then had to stand behind her
doing nothing while she rummaged among various little
bottles; moreover, when she turned around she was
startled, a bottle fell on the floor and broke, a splinter
of glass wounded Gregor in the face, some kind of corrosive medicine flowed around him; now without waiting
any longer, Grete grabbed as many little bottles as she
could carry and ran with them inside to her mother;
she slammed the door behind her with her foot. Now
Gregor was cut off from his mother, who was perhaps
near death through his fault; he could not dare open
the door if he did not want to chase away his sister,

who had to stay with his mother; now there was nothing for him to do except wait; and tormented by self-reproaches and worry, he began to crawl, crawled over everything, walls, furniture and ceiling, and finally in desperation, as the whole room was beginning to spin, fell down onto the middle of the big table.

A short time passed; Gregor lay there prostrate; all around, things were quiet, perhaps that was a good sign. Then the doorbell rang. The maid, of course, was locked up in her kitchen and so Grete had to answer the door. His father had come home. "What's happened?" were his first words; Grete's appearance must have told him everything. Grete answered in a muffled voice, her face was obviously pressed against her father's chest; "Mother fainted, but she's better now. Gregor's broken out." "I knew it," his father said. "I kept telling you, but you women don't want to listen." It was clear to Gregor that his father had put the worst interpretation on Grete's all-too-brief announcement and assumed that Gregor was guilty of some outrage. Therefore Gregor now had to try to calm his father down, since he had neither the time nor the ability to enlighten him. And so he fled to the door of his room and pressed himself against it for his father to see, as soon as he came into the foyer, that Gregor had the best intentions of returning to his room immediately and that it was not necessary to drive him back; if only the door were opened for him, he would disappear at once.

But his father was in no mood to notice such subtleties; "Ah!" he cried as he entered, in a tone that sounded as if he were at once furious and glad. Gregor turned his head away from the door and lifted it toward his father. He had not really imagined his father looking like this, as he stood in front of him now; admittedly Gregor had been too absorbed recently in his newfangled crawling to bother as much as before about events in the rest of the house and should really have been prepared to find some changes. And yet, and yet—was this still his father? Was this the same man who in the old days used to lie wearily buried in bed when Gregor left on a business

trip; who greeted him on his return in the evening,
sitting in his bathrobe in the armchair, who actually had
difficulty getting to his feet but as a sign of joy only
lifted up his arms; and who, on the rare occasions when
the whole family went out for a walk, on a few Sundays
in June and on the major holidays, used to shuffle along
with great effort between Gregor and his mother, who
were slow walkers themselves, always a little more
slowly than they, wrapped in his old overcoat, always
carefully planting down his crutch-handled cane, and,
when he wanted to say something, nearly always stood
still and assembled his escort around him? Now, however, he was holding himself very erect, dressed in a
tight-fitting blue uniform with gold buttons, the kind
worn by messengers at banking concerns; above the high
stiff collar of the jacket his heavy chin protruded; under
his bushy eyebrows his black eyes darted bright, piercing
glances; his usually rumpled white hair was combed flat,
with a scrupulously exact, gleaming part. He threw his
cap—which was adorned with a gold monogram, probably
that of a bank—in an arc across the entire room onto the
couch, and with the tails of his long uniform jacket
slapped back, his hands in his pants pockets, went for
Gregor with a sullen look on his face. He probably did
not know himself what he had in mind; still he lifted his
feet unusually high off the floor, and Gregor staggered at
the gigantic size of the soles of his boots. But he did not
linger over this, he had known right from the first day of
his new life that his father considered only the strictest
treatment called for in dealing with him. And so he ran
ahead of his father, stopped when his father stood still,
and scooted ahead again when his father made even the
slightest movement. In this way they made more than one
tour of the room, without anything decisive happening; in
fact the whole movement did not even have the appearance of a chase because of its slow tempo. So Gregor kept
to the floor for the time being, especially since he was
afraid that his father might interpret a flight onto the
walls or the ceiling as a piece of particular nastiness. Of
course Gregor had to admit that he would not be able to

keep up even this running for long, for whenever his father took one step, Gregor had to execute countless movements. He was already beginning to feel winded, just as in the old days he had not had very reliable lungs. As he now staggered around, hardly keeping his eyes open in order to gather all his strength for the running; in his obtuseness not thinking of any escape other than by running; and having almost forgotten that the walls were at his disposal, though here of course they were blocked up with elaborately carved furniture full of notches and points—at that moment a lightly flung object hit the floor right near him and rolled in front of him. It was an apple; a second one came flying right after it; Gregor stopped dead with fear; further running was useless, for his father was determined to bombard him. He had filled his pockets from the fruit bowl on the buffet and was now pitching one apple after another, for the time being without taking good aim. These little red apples rolled around on the floor as if electrified, clicking into each another. One apple, thrown weakly, grazed Gregor's back and slid off harmlessly. But the very next one that came flying after it literally forced its way into Gregor's back; Gregor tried to drag himself away, as if the startling, unbelievable pain might disappear with a change of place; but he felt nailed to the spot and stretched out his body in a complete confusion of all his senses. With his last glance he saw the door of his room burst open as his mother rushed out ahead of his screaming sister, in her chemise, for his sister had partly undressed her while she was unconscious in order to let her breathe more freely; saw his mother run up to his father and on the way her unfastened petticoats slide to the floor one by one; and saw as, stumbling over the skirts, she forced herself onto his father, and embracing him, in complete union with him—but now Gregor's sight went dim—her hands clasping his father's neck, begged for Gregor's life.

III

Gregor's serious wound, from which he suffered for over a month—the apple remained imbedded in his flesh as a visible souvenir since no one dared to remove it—seemed to have reminded even his father that Gregor was a member of the family, in spite of his present pathetic and repulsive shape, who could not be treated as an enemy; that, on the contrary, it was the commandment of family duty to swallow their disgust and endure him, endure him and nothing more.

And now, although Gregor had lost some of his mobility probably for good because of his wound, and although for the time being he needed long, long minutes to get across his room, like an old war veteran—crawling above ground was out of the question—for this deterioration of his situation he was granted compensation which in his view was entirely satisfactory: every day around dusk the living-room door—which he was in the habit of watching closely for an hour or two beforehand—was opened, so that, lying in the darkness of his room, invisible from the living room, he could see the whole family sitting at the table under the lamp and could listen to their conversation, as it were with general permission; and so it was completely different from before.

Of course these were no longer the animated conversations of the old days, which Gregor used to remember with a certain nostalgia in small hotel rooms when he'd had to throw himself wearily into the damp bedding. Now things were mostly very quiet. Soon after supper his father would fall asleep in his armchair; his mother and sister would caution each other to be quiet; his mother, bent low under the light, sewed delicate lingerie for a clothing store; his sister, who had taken a job as a salesgirl, was learning shorthand and French in the evenings in order to attain a better position some time in the future. Sometimes his father woke up, and as if he had absolutely no idea that he had been asleep, said to his mother, "Look how long you're sewing again today!" and went right back to sleep, while mother and sister smiled wearily at each other.

With a kind of perverse obstinacy his father refused to take off his official uniform even in the house; and while his robe hung uselessly on the clothes hook, his father dozed, completely dressed, in his chair, as if he were always ready for duty and were waiting even here for the voice of his superior. As a result his uniform, which had not been new to start with, began to get dirty in spite of all the mother's and sister's care, and Gregor would often stare all evening long at this garment, covered with stains and gleaming with its constantly polished gold buttons, in which the old man slept most uncomfortably and yet peacefully.

As soon as the clock struck ten, his mother tried to awaken his father with soft encouraging words and then persuade him to go to bed, for this was no place to sleep properly, and his father badly needed his sleep, since he had to be at work at six o'clock. But with the obstinacy that had possessed him ever since he had become a messenger, he always insisted on staying at the table a little longer, although he invariably fell asleep and then could be persuaded only with the greatest effort to exchange his armchair for bed. However much mother and sister might pounce on him with little admonitions, he would slowly shake his head for a quarter of an hour at a time, keeping his eyes closed, and would not get up. Gregor's mother plucked him by the sleeves, whispered blandishments into his ear, his sister dropped her homework in order to help her mother, but all this was of no use. He only sank deeper into his armchair. Not until the women lifted him up under his arms did he open his eyes, look alternately at mother and sister, and usually say, "What a life. So this is the peace of my old age." And leaning on the two women, he would get up laboriously, as if he were the greatest weight on himself, and let the women lead him to the door, where, shrugging them off, he would proceed independently, while Gregor's mother threw down her sewing and his sister her pen as quickly as possible so as to run after his father and be of further assistance.

Who in this overworked and exhausted family had time to worry about Gregor any more than was absolutely necessary? The household was stinted more and more; now the maid was let go after all; a gigantic bony cleaning woman with white hair fluttering about her head came mornings and evenings to do the heaviest work; his mother took care of everything else, along with all her sewing. It even happened that various pieces of family jewelry, which in the old days his mother and sister had been overjoyed to wear at parties and celebrations, were sold, as Gregor found out one evening from the general discussion of the prices they had fetched. But the biggest complaint was always that they could not give up the apartment, which was much too big for their present needs, since no one could figure out how Gregor was supposed to be moved. But Gregor understood easily that it was not only consideration for him which prevented their moving, for he could easily have been transported in a suitable crate with a few air holes; what mainly prevented the family from moving was their complete hopelessness and the thought that they had been struck by a misfortune as none of their relatives and acquaintances had ever been hit. What the world demands of poor people they did to the utmost of their ability; his father brought breakfast for the minor officials at the bank, his mother sacrificed herself to the underwear of strangers, his sister ran back and forth behind the counter at the request of the customers; but for anything more than this they did not have the strength. And the wound in Gregor's back began to hurt anew when mother and sister, after getting his father to bed, now came back, dropped their work, pulled their chairs close to each other and sat cheek to cheek; when his mother, pointing to Gregor's room, said, "Close that door, Grete"; and when Gregor was back in darkness, while in the other room the women mingled their tears or stared dry-eyed at the table.

Gregor spent the days and nights almost entirely without sleep. Sometimes he thought that the next time the door opened he would take charge of the family's affairs again, just as he had done in the old days; after this long while there again appeared in his thoughts the boss and the manager, the salesmen and the trainees, the handyman who was so dense, two or three friends from other firms, a chambermaid in a provincial hotel—a happy fleeting memory—a cashier in a millinery store, whom he had courted earnestly but too slowly—they all appeared, intermingled with strangers or people he had already forgotten; but instead of helping him and his family, they were all inaccessible, and he was glad when they faded away. At other times he was in no mood to worry about his family, he was completely filled with rage at his miserable treatment, and although he could not imagine anything that would pique his appetite, he still made plans for getting into the pantry to take what was coming to him, even if he wasn't hungry. No longer considering what she could do to give Gregor a special treat, his sister, before running to business every morning and afternoon, hurriedly shoved any old food into Gregor's room with her foot; and in the evening, regardless of whether the food had only been toyed with or—the most usual case—had been left completely untouched, she swept it out with a swish of the broom. The cleaning up of Gregor's room, which she now always did in the evenings, could not be done more hastily. Streaks of dirt ran along the walls, fluffs of dust and filth lay here and there on the floor. At first, whenever his sister came in, Gregor would place himself in those corners which were particularly offending, meaning by his position in a sense to reproach her. But he could probably have stayed there for weeks without his sister's showing any improvement; she must have seen the dirt as clearly as he did, but she had just decided to leave it. At the same time she made sure—with an irritableness that was completely new to her and which had in fact infected the whole family—

that the cleaning of Gregor's room remain her province. One time his mother had submitted Gregor's room to a major housecleaning, which she managed only after employing a couple of pails of water—all this dampness, of course, irritated Gregor too and he lay prostrate, sour and immobile, on the couch—but his mother's punishment was not long in coming. For hardly had his sister noticed the difference in Gregor's room that evening than, deeply insulted, she ran into the living room and, in spite of her mother's imploringly uplifted hands, burst out in a fit of crying, which his parents—his father had naturally been startled out of his armchair—at first watched in helpless amazement; until they too got going; turning to the right, his father blamed his mother for not letting his sister clean Gregor's room; but turning to the left, he screamed at his sister that she would never again be allowed to clean Gregor's room; while his mother tried to drag his father, who was out of his mind with excitement, into the bedroom; his sister, shaken with sobs, hammered the table with her small fists; and Gregor hissed loudly with rage because it did not occur to any of them to close the door and spare him such a scene and a row.

But even if his sister, exhausted from her work at the store, had gotten fed up with taking care of Gregor as she used to, it was not necessary at all for his mother to take her place and still Gregor did not have to be neglected. For now the cleaning woman was there. This old widow, who thanks to her strong bony frame had probably survived the worst in a long life, was not really repelled by Gregor. Without being in the least inquisitive, she had once accidentally opened the door of Gregor's room, and at the sight of Gregor—who, completely taken by surprise, began to race back and forth although no one was chasing him—she had remained standing, with her hands folded on her stomach, marveling. From that time on she never failed to open the door a crack every morning and every evening and peek in hurriedly at Gregor. In the beginning she also used to call him over to her with words she probably considered friendly, like,

"Come over here for a minute, you old dung beetle!" or "Look at that old dung beetle!" To forms of address like these Gregor would not respond but remained immobile where he was, as if the door had not been opened. If only they had given this cleaning woman orders to clean up his room every day, instead of letting her disturb him uselessly whenever the mood took her. Once, early in the morning—heavy rain, perhaps already a sign of approaching spring, was beating on the window panes—Gregor was so exasperated when the cleaning woman started in again with her phrases that he turned on her, of course slowly and decrepitly, as if to attack. But the cleaning woman, instead of getting frightened, simply lifted up high a chair near the door, and as she stood there with her mouth wide open, her intention was clearly to shut her mouth only when the chair in her hand came crashing down on Gregor's back. "So, is that all there is?" she asked when Gregor turned around again, and she quietly put the chair back in the corner.

Gregor now hardly ate anything anymore. Only when he accidentally passed the food laid out for him would he take a bite into his mouth just for fun, hold it in for hours, and then mostly spit it out again. At first he thought that his grief at the state of his room kept him off food, but it was the very changes in his room to which he quickly became adjusted. His family had gotten into the habit of putting in this room things for which they could not find any other place, and now there were plenty of these, since one of the rooms in the apartment had been rented to three boarders. These serious gentlemen —all three had long beards, as Gregor was able to register once through a crack in the door—were obsessed with neatness, not only in their room, but since they had, after all, moved in here, throughout the entire household and especially in the kitchen. They could not stand useless, let alone dirty junk. Besides, they had brought along most of their own household goods. For this reason many things had become superfluous, and though they certainly weren't salable, on the other hand they could not just be thrown out. All these things migrated into Gregor's

room. Likewise the ash can and the garbage can from
the kitchen. Whatever was not being used at the moment
was just flung into Gregor's room by the cleaning woman,
who was always in a big hurry; fortunately Gregor generally saw only the object involved and the hand that
held it. Maybe the cleaning woman intended to reclaim
the things as soon as she had a chance or else to throw
out everything together in one fell swoop, but in fact
they would have remained lying wherever they had
been thrown in the first place if Gregor had not squeezed
through the junk and set it in motion, at first from necessity, because otherwise there would have been no room
to crawl in, but later with growing pleasure, although
after such excursions, tired to death and sad, he did
not budge again for hours.

Since the roomers sometimes also had their supper at
home in the common living room, the living-room door remained closed on certain evenings, but Gregor found it
very easy to give up the open door, for on many evenings
when it was opened he had not taken advantage of it, but
instead, without the family's noticing, had lain in the
darkest corner of his room. But once the cleaning woman
had left the living-room door slightly open, and it also
remained opened a little when the roomers came in
in the evening and the lamp was lit. They sat down at
the head of the table where in the old days his father,
his mother, and Gregor had eaten,* unfolded their nap-
kins, and picked up their knives and forks. At once his
mother appeared in the doorway with a platter of meat,
and just behind her came his sister with a platter piled
high with potatoes. A thick vapor steamed up from the
food. The roomers bent over the platters set in front of
them as if to examine them before eating, and in fact the
one who sat in the middle, and who seemed to be regarded by the other two as an authority, cut into a piece
of meat while it was still on the platter, evidently to find
out whether it was tender enough or whether it should
perhaps be sent back to the kitchen. He was satisfied, and

---

* had sat,

mother and sister, who had been watching anxiously, sighed with relief and began to smile.

The family itself ate in the kitchen. Nevertheless, before going into the kitchen, his father came into this room and, bowing once, cap in hand, made a turn around the table. The roomers rose as one man and mumbled something into their beards. When they were alone again, they ate in almost complete silence. It seemed strange to Gregor that among all the different noises of eating he kept picking up the sound of their chewing teeth, as if this were a sign to Gregor that you needed teeth to eat with and that even with the best make of toothless jaws you couldn't do a thing. "I'm hungry enough," Gregor said to himself, full of grief, "but not for these things. Look how these roomers are gorging themselves, and I'm dying!"

On this same evening—Gregor could not remember having heard the violin during the whole time—the sound of violin playing came from the kitchen. The roomers had already finished their evening meal, the one in the middle had taken out a newspaper, given each of the two others a page, and now, leaning back, they read and smoked. When the violin began to play, they became attentive, got up, and went on tiptoe to the door leading to the foyer, where they stood in a huddle. They must have been heard in the kitchen, for his father called, "Perhaps the playing bothers you, gentlemen? It can be stopped right away." "On the contrary," said the middle roomer. "Wouldn't the young lady like to come in to us and play in here where it's much roomier and more comfortable?" "Oh, certainly," called Gregor's father, as if he were the violinist. The boarders went back into the room and waited. Soon Gregor's father came in with the music stand, his mother with the sheet music, and his sister with the violin. Calmly his sister got everything ready for playing; his parents—who had never rented out rooms before and therefore behaved toward the roomers with excessive politeness—did not even dare sit down on their own chairs; his father leaned against the door, his right hand inserted between two buttons of his uni-

form coat, which he kept closed; but his mother was
offered a chair by one of the roomers, and since she left
the chair where the roomer just happened to put it, she
sat in a corner to one side.

His sister began to play. Father and mother, from
either side, attentively followed the movements of her
hands. Attracted by the playing, Gregor had dared to
come out a little further and already had his head in
the living room. It hardly surprised him that lately he
was showing so little consideration for the others; once
such consideration had been his greatest pride. And yet
he would never have had better reason to keep hidden;
for now, because of the dust which lay all over his room
and blew around at the slightest movement, he too was
completely covered with dust; he dragged around with
him on his back and along his sides fluff and hairs and
scraps of food; his indifference to everything was much
too deep for him to have gotten on his back and scrubbed
himself clean against the carpet, as once he had done
several times a day. And in spite of his state, he was not
ashamed to inch out a little farther on the immaculate
living-room floor.

Admittedly no one paid any attention to him. The
family was completely absorbed by the violin-playing;
the roomers, on the other hand, who at first had stationed
themselves, hands in pockets, much too close behind his
sister's music stand, so that they could all have followed
the score, which certainly must have upset his sister, soon
withdrew to the window, talking to each other in an
undertone, their heads lowered, where they remained,
anxiously watched by his father. It now seemed only too
obvious that they were disappointed in their expectation
of hearing beautiful or entertaining violin-playing, had
had enough of the whole performance and continued to
let their peace be disturbed only out of politeness. Especially the way they all blew the cigar smoke out of their
nose and mouth toward the ceiling suggested great
nervousness. And yet his sister was playing so beautifully.
Her face was inclined to one side, sadly and probingly
her eyes followed the lines of music. Gregor crawled

forward a little farther, holding his head close to the floor, so that it might be possible to catch her eye. Was he an animal, that music could move him so? He felt as if the way to the unknown nourishment he longed for were coming to light. He was determined to force himself on until he reached his sister, to pluck at her skirt, and to let her know in this way that she should bring her violin into his room, for no one here appreciated her playing the way he would appreciate it. He would never again let her out of his room—at least not for as long as he lived; for once, his nightmarish looks would be of use to him; he would be at all the doors of his room at the same time and hiss and spit at the aggressors; his sister, however, should not be forced to stay with him, but would do so of her own free will; she should sit next to him on the couch, bending her ear down to him, and then he would confide to her that he had had the firm intention of sending her to the Conservatory, and that, if the catastrophe had not intervened, he would have announced this to everyone last Christmas—certainly Christmas had come and gone?—without taking notice of any objections. After this declaration his sister would burst into tears of emotion, and Gregor would raise himself up to her shoulder and kiss her on the neck which, ever since she started going out to work, she kept bare, without a ribbon or collar.

"Mr. Samsa!" the middle roomer called to Gregor's father and without wasting another word pointed his index finger at Gregor, who was slowly moving forward. The violin stopped, the middle roomer smiled first at his friends, shaking his head, and then looked at Gregor again. Rather than driving Gregor out, his father seemed to consider it more urgent to start by soothing the roomers although they were not at all upset, and Gregor seemed to be entertaining them more than the violin-playing. He rushed over to them and tried with outstretched arms to drive them into their room and at the same time with his body to block their view of Gregor. Now they actually did get a little angry—it was not clear whether because of his father's behavior or because of their dawning re-

alization of having had without knowing it such a next
door neighbor as Gregor. They demanded explanations
from his father; in their turn they raised their arms,
plucked excitedly at their beards, and, dragging their
feet, backed off toward their room. In the meantime his
sister had overcome the abstracted mood into which she
had fallen after her playing had been so suddenly interrupted; and all at once, after holding violin and bow for
a while in her slackly hanging hands and continuing to
follow the score as if she were still playing, she pulled
herself together, laid the instrument on the lap of her
mother—who was still sitting in her chair, fighting for
breath, her lungs violently heaving—and ran into the
next room, which the roomers, under pressure from her
father, were nearing more quickly than before. One could
see the covers and bolsters on the beds, obeying his
sister's practiced hands, fly up and arrange themselves.
Before the boarders had reached the room, she had
finished turning down the beds and had slipped out.
Her father seemed once again to be gripped by his perverse obstinacy to such a degree that he completely forgot
any respect still due his tenants. He drove them on and
kept on driving until, already at the bedroom door, the
middle boarder stamped his foot thunderingly and thus
brought him to a standstill. "I herewith declare," he said,
raising his hand and casting his eyes around for Gregor's
mother and sister too, "that in view of the disgusting
conditions prevailing in this apartment and family"—
here he spat curtly and decisively on the floor—"I give
notice as of now. Of course I won't pay a cent for the
days I have been living here, either; on the contrary, I
shall consider taking some sort of action against you
with claims that—believe me—will be easy to substan-
tiate." He stopped and looked straight in front of him,
as if he were expecting something. And in fact his two
friends at once chimed in with the words, "We too give
notice as of now." Thereupon he grabbed the door knob
and slammed the door with a bang.

Gregor's father, his hands groping, staggered to his
armchair and collapsed into it; it looked as if he were

stretching himself out for his usual evening nap, but the heavy drooping of his head, as if it had lost all support, showed that he was certainly not asleep. All this time Gregor had lain quietly at the spot where the roomers had surprised him. His disappointment at the failure of his plan—but perhaps also the weakness caused by so much fasting—made it impossible for him to move. He was afraid with some certainty that in the very next moment a general debacle would burst over him, and he waited. He was not even startled by the violin as it slipped from under his mother's trembling fingers and fell off her lap with a reverberating clang.

"My dear parents," said his sister and by way of an introduction pounded her hand on the table, "things can't go on like this. Maybe you don't realize it, but I do. I won't pronounce the name of my brother in front of this monster, and so all I say is: we have to try to get rid of it. We've done everything humanly possible to take care of it and to put up with it; I don't think anyone can blame us in the least."

"She's absolutely right," said his father to himself. His mother, who still could not catch her breath, began to cough dully behind her hand, a wild look in her eyes.

His sister rushed over to his mother and held her forehead. His father seemed to have been led by Grete's words to more definite thoughts, had sat up, was playing with the cap of his uniform among the plates which were still lying * on the table from the roomers' supper, and from time to time looked at Gregor's motionless form.

"We must try to get rid of it," his sister now said exclusively to her father, since her mother was coughing too hard to hear anything. "It will be the death of you two, I can see it coming. People who already have to work as hard as we do can't put up with this constant torture at home, too. I can't stand it anymore either." And she broke out crying so bitterly that her tears poured down onto her mother's face, which she wiped off with mechanical movements of her hand.

---

* standing.

"Child," said her father kindly and with unusual understanding, "but what can we do?"

Gregor's sister only shrugged her shoulders as a sign of the bewildered mood that had now gripped her as she cried, in contrast with her earlier confidence.

"If he could understand us," said her father, half questioning; in the midst of her crying Gregor's sister waved her hand violently as a sign that that was out of the question.

"If he could understand us," his father repeated and by closing his eyes, absorbed his daughter's conviction of the impossibility of the idea, "then maybe we could come to an agreement with him. But the way things are———"

"It has to go," cried his sister. "That's the only answer, Father. You just have to try to get rid of the idea that it's Gregor. Believing it for so long, that is our real misfortune. But how can it be Gregor? If it were Gregor, he would have realized long ago that it isn't possible for human beings to live with such a creature, and he would have gone away of his own free will. Then we wouldn't have a brother, but we'd be able to go on living and honor his memory. But as things are, this animal persecutes us, drives the roomers away, obviously wants to occupy the whole apartment and for us to sleep in the gutter. Look, Father," she suddenly shrieked, "he's starting in again!" And in a fit of terror that was completely incomprehensible to Gregor, his sister abandoned even her mother, literally shoved herself off from her chair, as if she would rather sacrifice her mother than stay near Gregor, and rushed behind her father, who, upset only by her behavior, also stood up and half-lifted his arms in front of her as if to protect her.

But Gregor had absolutely no intention of frightening anyone, let alone his sister. He had only begun to turn around in order to trek back to his room; certainly his movements did look peculiar, since his ailing condition made him help the complicated turning maneuver along with his head, which he lifted up many times and knocked against the floor. He stopped and looked around. His good intention seemed to have been recognized; it had only been a momentary scare. Now they all watched him, silent and sad. His mother lay in her armchair, her legs stretched out and pressed together, her eyes almost closing from exhaustion; his father and his sister sat side by side, his sister had put her arm around her father's neck.

Now maybe they'll let me turn around, Gregor thought and began his labors again. He could not repress his panting from the exertion, and from time to time he had to rest. Otherwise no one harassed him, he was left completely on his own. When he had completed the turn, he immediately began to crawl back in a straight line. He was astonished at the great distance separating him from his room and could not understand at all how, given his weakness, he had covered the same distance a little while ago almost without realizing it. Constantly intent only on rapid crawling, he hardly noticed that not a word, not an exclamation from his family interrupted him. Only when he was already in the doorway did he turn his head—not completely, for he felt his neck stiffening; nevertheless he still saw that behind him nothing had changed except that his sister had gotten up. His last glance ranged over his mother, who was now fast asleep.

He was hardly inside his room when the door was hurriedly slammed shut, firmly bolted, and locked. Gregor was so frightened at the sudden noise behind him that his little legs gave way under him. It was his sister who had been in such a hurry. She had been standing up straight, ready and waiting, then she had leaped forward nimbly, Gregor had not even heard her coming, and she cried "Finally!" to her parents as she turned the key in the lock.

"And now?" Gregor asked himself, looking around in the darkness. He soon made the discovery that he could no longer move at all. It did not surprise him; rather, it seemed unnatural that until now he had actually been able to propel himself on these thin little legs. Otherwise he felt relatively comfortable. He had pains, of course, throughout his whole body, but it seemed to him that they were gradually getting fainter and fainter and would finally go away altogether. The rotten apple in his back and the inflamed area around it, which were completely covered with fluffy dust, already hardly bothered him. He thought back on his family with deep emotion and love. His conviction that he would have to disappear was, if possible, even firmer than his sister's. He remained in this state of empty and peaceful reflection until the tower clock struck three in the morning. He still saw that outside the window everything was beginning to grow light. Then, without his consent, his head sank down to the floor, and from his nostrils streamed his last weak breath.

When early in the morning the cleaning woman came—in sheer energy and impatience she would slam all the doors so hard although she had often been asked not to, that once she had arrived, quiet sleep was no longer possible anywhere in the apartment—she did not at first find anything out of the ordinary on paying Gregor her usual short visit. She thought that he was deliberately lying motionless, pretending that his feelings were hurt; she credited him with unlimited intelligence. Because she happened to be holding the long broom, she tried from the doorway to tickle Gregor with it. When this too produced no results, she became annoyed and jabbed Gregor a little, and only when she had shoved him without any resistance to another spot did she begin to take notice. When she quickly became aware of the true state of things, she opened her eyes wide, whistled softly, but did not dawdle; instead, she tore open the door of the bedroom and shouted at the top of her voice into the darkness: "Come and have a look, it's croaked; it's lying there, dead as a doornail!"

The couple Mr. and Mrs. Samsa sat up in their marriage bed and had a struggle overcoming their shock at the cleaning woman before they could finally grasp her message. But then Mr. and Mrs. Samsa hastily scrambled out of bed, each on his side, Mr. Samsa threw the blanket around his shoulders, Mrs. Samsa came out in nothing but her nightgown; dressed this way, they entered Gregor's room. In the meantime the door of the living room had also opened, where Grete had been sleeping since the roomers had moved in; she was fully dressed, as if she had not been asleep at all; and her pale face seemed to confirm this. "Dead?" said Mrs. Samsa and looked inquiringly at the cleaning woman, although she could scrutinize everything for herself and could recognize the truth even without scrutiny. "I'll say," said the cleaning woman, and to prove it she pushed Gregor's corpse with her broom a good distance sideways. Mrs. Samsa made a movement as if to hold the broom back but did not do it. "Well," said Mr. Samsa, "now we can thank God!" He crossed himself, and the three women followed his example. Grete, who never took her eyes off the corpse, said, "Just look how thin he was. Of course he didn't eat anything for such a long time. The food came out again just the way it went in." As a matter of fact, Gregor's body was completely flat and dry; this was obvious now for the first time, really, since the body was no longer raised up by his little legs and nothing else distracted the eye.

"Come in with us for a little while, Grete," said Mrs. Samsa with a melancholy smile, and Grete, not without looking back at the corpse, followed her parents into their bedroom. The cleaning woman shut the door and opened the window wide. Although it was early in the morning, there was already some mildness mixed in with the fresh air. After all, it was already the end of March.

The three boarders came out of their room and looked around in astonishment for their breakfast; they had been forgotten. "Where's breakfast?" the middle roomer grumpily asked the cleaning woman. But she put her finger to her lips and then hastily and silently beckoned the boarders to follow her into Gregor's room. They came willingly and then stood, their hands in the pockets of their somewhat shabby jackets, in the now already very bright room, surrounding Gregor's corpse.

At that point the bedroom door opened, and Mr. Samsa appeared in his uniform, his wife on one arm, his daughter on the other. They all looked as if they had been crying; from time to time Grete pressed her face against her father's sleeve.

"Leave my house immediately," said Mr. Samsa and pointed to the door, without letting go of the women. "What do you mean by that?" said the middle roomer, somewhat nonplussed, and smiled with a sugary smile. The two others held their hands behind their back and incessantly rubbed them together, as if in joyful anticipation of a big argument, which could only turn out in their favor. "I mean just what I say," answered Mr. Samsa and with his two companions marched in a straight line toward the roomer. At first the roomer stood still and looked at the floor, as if the thoughts inside his head were fitting themselves together in a new order. "So, we'll go, then," he said and looked up at Mr. Samsa as if, suddenly overcome by a fit of humility, he were asking for further permission even for this decision. Mr. Samsa merely nodded briefly several times, his eyes wide open. Thereupon the roomer actually went immediately into the foyer, taking long strides; his two friends had already been listening for a while, their hands completely still, and now they went hopping right after him, as if afraid that Mr. Samsa might get into the foyer ahead of them and interrupt the contact with their leader. In the foyer all three took their hats from the coatrack, pulled their canes from the umbrella stand, bowed silently, and left the apartment. In a suspicious mood which proved completely unfounded, Mr. Samsa led the two women out onto the landing; leaning over the banister, they watched the three roomers slowly but steadily going down the long flight of stairs, disappearing on each landing at a particular turn of the stairway and a few moments later emerging again; the farther down they got, the more the Samsa family's interest in them wore off, and when a butcher's boy with a carrier on his head came climbing up the stairs with a proud bearing, toward them and then up on past them, Mr. Samsa and the women quickly left the banister and all went back, as if relieved, into their apartment.

They decided to spend this day resting and going for a walk; they not only deserved a break in their work, they absolutely needed one. And so they sat down at the table and wrote three letters of excuse, Mr. Samsa to the management of the bank, Mrs. Samsa to her employer, and Grete to the store owner. While they were writing, the cleaning woman came in to say that she was going, since her morning's work was done. The three letter writers at first simply nodded without looking up, but as the cleaning woman still kept lingering, they looked up, annoyed. "Well?" asked Mr. Samsa. The cleaning woman stood smiling in the doorway, as if she had some great good news to announce to the family but would do so only if she were thoroughly questioned. The little ostrich feather which stood almost upright on her hat and which had irritated Mr. Samsa the whole time she had been with them swayed lightly in all directions. "What do you want?" asked Mrs. Samsa, who inspired the most respect in the cleaning woman. "Well," the cleaning woman answered, and for good-natured laughter could not immediately go on, "look, you don't have to worry about getting rid of the stuff next door. It's already been taken care of." Mrs. Samsa and Grete bent down over their letters, as if to continue writing; Mr. Samsa, who noticed that the cleaning woman was now about to start describing everything in detail, stopped her with a firmly outstretched hand. But since she was not going to be permitted to tell her story, she remembered that she was in a great hurry, cried, obviously insulted, "So long, everyone," whirled around wildly, and left the apartment with a terrible slamming of doors.

"We'll fire her tonight," said Mr. Samsa, but did not get an answer from either his wife or his daughter, for the cleaning woman seemed to have ruined their barely regained peace of mind. They got up, went to the window, and stayed there, holding each other tight. Mr. Samsa turned around in his chair toward them and watched them quietly for a while. Then he called, "Come on now, come over here. Stop brooding over the past. And have a little consideration for me, too." The women obeyed him at once, hurried over to him, fondled him, and quickly finished their letters.

Then all three of them left the apartment together, something they had not done in months, and took the trolley into the open country on the outskirts of the city. The car, in which they were the only passengers, was completely filled with warm sunshine. Leaning back comfortably in their seats, they discussed their prospects for the time to come, and it seemed on closer examination that these weren't bad at all, for all three positions— about which they had never really asked one another in any detail—were exceedingly advantageous and especially promising for the future. The greatest immediate improvement in their situation would come easily, of course, from a change in apartments; they would now take a smaller and cheaper apartment, but one better situated and in every way simpler to manage than the old one, which Gregor had picked for them. While they were talking in this vein, it occurred almost simultaneously to Mr. and Mrs. Samsa, as they watched their daughter getting livelier and livelier, that lately, in spite of all the troubles * which had turned her cheeks pale, she had blossomed into a good-looking, shapely girl. Growing quieter and communicating almost unconsciously through glances, they thought that it would soon be time, too, to find her a good husband. And it was like a confirmation of their new dreams and good intentions when at the end of the ride their daughter got up first and stretched her young body.

---

* care [i.e., cosmetic]

A Note on the Text

Die Verwandlung (*The Metamorphosis*) first appeared in 1915 in the journal *Die weissen Blätter,* volumes ten to twelve. Kafka did not correct the proofs of this edition, which contains many printer's errors.

This translation is based on the first book edition of *Die Verwandlung,* double volume 22/23 in the series "Der jüngste Tag" with a cover illustration by Ottomar Starke, published in Leipzig by the Kurt Wolff Verlag in November, 1915. The German text has recently been reissued in a facsimile edition: *Der jüngste Tag, Die Bücherei einer Epoche,* edited by Heinz Schöffler, two volumes (Frankfurt am Main: Verlag Heinrich Scheffler, 1970).

A second edition of *Die Verwandlung* was brought out by the Kurt Wolff Verlag in 1917, but it is difficult to decide whether Kafka had a hand in this version. I count fifty-seven changes between this edition and the edition of 1915, of which I judge eleven to be degradations, ten to be improvements, and the rest of minimal consequence. The very few variants that alter the sense of the text (the vast majority of the changes are concerned with orthography and punctuation) have been incorporated in footnotes to this translation.

EXPLANATORY NOTES
TO THE TEXT

Numbers in italic refer to page numbers of this edition.

Numbers in roman refer to page numbers of the work cited.

The Metamorphosis (*Die Verwandlung*)

For Weinberg, who explores the underlying religious symbolism of this story, Gregor Samsa's transformation is quite literally a *"negative transfiguration,* the inversion of the Transfiguration of Christ, the Passion of an abortive Christ figure. . . . If this is the case," Weinberg continues, "then instead of *Metamorphosis . . . Die Verwandlung* would have to be translated, in the spirit of Kafka, faithfully and ironically, as *The Transfiguration . . .* indeed, even as *The Transsubstantiation . . ."* (257–58). Politzer maintains, however, that Kafka's religious innuendos throughout *The Metamorphosis* are no more than "a literary play with the religious connotation of his images"; their denotation lies elsewhere (73).

Kafka's deepest concern in 1912 is for literature and not for religion, for the time to write, the hope of writing well, and the exalted states that flowed from his advancing a little on this way.* Kafka's masters are Goethe and Flaubert rather than the rabbis, the Prophets as poets rather than as theologians. In 1912 he does not study religion (least of all the Catholicism which upholds transsubstantiation) either as an idea in cultural history or as a practical basis for belief. His "Messianic" hopes address a reconciliation of the opposing demands of literature and the "law"—the law according to which that man is saved who marries, has children, and takes up a profession binding him to the community; a law, in short, prescribing secular means to secular salvation.†

The title of this story should therefore not be *The Transsubstantiation. The Metamorphosis* captures the abrupt and uncanny character of the change and incidentally denotes the development of the sacred scarab (see Holland, 148). Freedman's wonderful suggestion is "The Changeling"; but this title has tendentious secondary meanings: it would fix

---

* The diary entry for November 15, 1911, is quite typical; it names literary inspiration as the source of that elevation (*Erhebung*) associated with religious experience.

† The relation between Kafka's literary and religious concerns is superbly analyzed by Blanchot.

the story into the genre of the fairy tale and characterize too whimsically the negative agency of Gregor's transformation. One meaning of the German title unfortunately goes astray in translation. *"Die Verwandlung"* is also the scene change on a theater stage.

Kassel calls attention to the title *The Metamorphosis* as meaning "the process of metamorphosis itself. But the story tells nothing of the process of the metamorphosis or its possible causes. It begins with a report of the fact of metamorphosis" (156).

Gregor Samsa

"Doubtless [the name Samsa] is a cryptogram for Kafka; but beyond this it is probably also a phonetic contraction of the Czech words *sám* ('alone') and *jsem* ('I am') = 'I am alone,' a cry of pain . . ." (Weinberg, 238).

Holland (149) explores the link Samsa-Samson.

unsettling dreams

"The 'unsettling dreams' from which Gregor awakens represent, so to speak, a final reminiscence by the story of that domain to which it owes its origin"—that is, the oneiric, the subconscious (Schlingmann, 91). See also Lecomte (61).

he found himself changed

A sign, for Schubiger, of the passivity of Gregor Samsa; he has not chosen his situation (28).

For Binion, this phrase is typical of the ambiguities running through the story which suggest that Gregor is not metamorphosed but only deluded. Binion equates narrator and hero, and writes of this phrase: "It falls within the narrative convention, corresponding as it does to the hero's ironic attitude toward his own symptoms" (217).

changed in his bed

A passage deleted by Kafka from *The Trial* reads: "As someone said to me—I can't remember now who it was—it is really remarkable that when you wake up in the morning you nearly always find everything in exactly the same place as the evening before. For when asleep and dreaming you are, apparently at least, in an essentially different state from that

of wakefulness; and therefore, as that man truly said, it
requires enormous presence of mind or rather quickness of
wit, when opening your eyes to seize hold as it were of everything in the room at exactly the same place where you had
let it go on the previous evening. That was why, he said,
the moment of waking up was the riskiest moment of the
day. Once that was well over without deflecting you from
your orbit, you could take heart of grace for the rest of the
day" (318–19).

The story opens with the collapse of this "riskiest moment"
into the metamorphosis. There are no empirical events leading
up to it, no attempts on Kafka's part to explain precisely why
it has occurred, in what sense the change is deserved or otherwise intelligible. The thrust of the work is to describe the
response of Gregor and his family to the abrupt metamorphosis
violently inserted into conventional reality. This idea is richly
developed by Schubiger (30) in conjunction with the passage
cited above.

Thus, as Greenberg points out, *The Metamorphosis* has its
climax in the opening sentence. The rest of the novella falls
off from its starting point, its high point. Here, evidently, the
traditional Aristotelian form of the narrative ceases to be
relevant. *The Metamorphosis* generates its form out of its
own fundamental subject matter: "The traditional kind of narrative based on the drama of dénouement—on the 'unknotting'
of complications and the coming to a conclusion—could not
serve Kafka because it is just exactly the absence of dénouement and conclusions that is his subject matter. His story is
about death, but death that is without dénouement, death
that is merely a spiritually inconclusive petering out" (70).

For Heselhaus the metamorphosis calls to mind the
Metamorphoses of Ovid. In Ovid, too, there is an insect
transformation: "Arachne, the artful weaver and worker, is
transformed into a spider by the angry Athene, as a punishment for her presumptuousness in having challenged the
goddess to a contest of their skills. But there is a decisive
difference between Ovid's Arachne story and Kafka's 'Metamorphosis': Kafka depicts the life and destiny of the being
who is metamorphosed—Ovid and classical writers depict only the act of metamorphosis" (363). See Ovid, VI,
1–145. But this "depiction" is anticlimactic: and in leaving the
metamorphosis unexplained, it introduces another distinction
between Kafka's and Ovid's fable.

monstrous vermin (*ungeheueres Ungeziefer*)

Weinberg notes that the linking of these two words is not fortuitous. *'Ungeziefer'* ["bug," "vermin"], a word in which undertones of the uncanny, the supernatural, the daemonic and also all possible conceptions of taboo vibrate in resonance, derives from the late Middle High German *ungezibere, unziver,* and originally meant the 'unclean animal not suited for sacrifice' (Grimm's *Deutsches Wörterbuch;* Kluge's *Etymologisches Wörterbuch der deutschen Sprache*). . . . As an adjective *'ungeheuer'* originally means much the same as *infamiliaris,* 'without a part in a family.' " Weinberg concludes: *"The 'sacrificial animal' regarded by his own kind as 'unclean' . . . is gradually denied the full part in family life which is his due"* (316–17).

Pong stresses "the terrifying character of an *'Un.'* It is the linguistic form of negation, which goes back to a dialectical process of separation" (263). See further Hasselblatt (193). Pongs noted earlier than Weinberg the highly charged etymological background of *"un-geheures Ungeziefer."* He comments: "The concentrated energy of Kafka's language . . . appears to be the only indication that Gregor is inwardly more deeply moved in his unconscious than his baldly registering language suggests" (263).

But Sokel attempts to preserve the entomological as well as the etymological identity of the *Ungeziefer* and suggests that Gregor is a cockroach. "The term 'vermin' holds the key to the double aspect of the metamorphosis. Vermin connotes something parasitic and aggressive, something that lives off human beings and may suck their blood; on the other hand, it connotes something defenseless, something that can be stepped on and crushed. Gregor's hugeness emphasizes the aggressive aspect. Moreover, at the beginning of the story the reader might be inclined to think of Gregor's new form as that [of] a bedbug. Kafka's famous letter to his father would give support to such a view since Kafka has his father refer to him as a blood-sucking type of vermin, a bedbug or a louse [*111*]. But later we discover that Gregor does not possess the aggressiveness of the blood-sucking vermin. He does not feed on blood, but on garbage. This diet (as well as the term 'Mistkäfer' [literally "dung beetle"; for Sokel, "cockroach"]) used by the charwoman and a later reference in Kafka's diary to 'the black beetle' of his story [*Diaries, I,* 304] lead one to believe that Gregor is akin to a cockroach, a creature that may nauseate human beings but does not attack them. Offensive in looks, it is defenseless in fact" ("Kafka's 'Metamorphosis,'" 213).

Empson's view is different: "[Gregor is] . . . a man-sized woodlouse . . . (he has more legs than a cockroach)." Luke describes the creature: "It is at least two feet wide, hard-backed, many-legged, brown, malodorous, eats household leavings at first but would perhaps prefer blood"; but he has already concluded that "the species of insect is not clearly stated" (43).

Politzer's view is the same, and it raises a crucial point: "The thoroughly negative quality of the transforming power seems to have been imparted to the animal itself. . . . The German word *Ungeziefer*, like its English equivalent 'vermin,' is a generic term, a collective noun denoting all sorts of undesirable insects. Kafka never divulges the kind of insect into which Gregor has been transformed, nor does he specify its form and size. In the beginning he is flat like a bedbug, so thin that he can find accommodation under the couch, and yet long enough to reach the door key with his teeth. It would stand to reason that he was changed into precisely that animal which he—and other European salesmen—dreaded most when they entered the cheap and dirty hotels open to them on their route. And yet there is no textual evidence to support Kafka's later claim that in 'The Metamorphosis' he was talking 'about the bedbugs in [his] own family' [110]. The *un-*, the dark, the void, are the only designations Kafka could find for the mystery at the center of the tale" (81).

Since the phrase "*ungeheueres Ungeziefer*" bears such a great weight of connotation in German, it is obviously impossible to translate satisfactorily into English. Among the previous translators of *The Metamorphosis*, Jolas renders it as "enormous bug"; Lloyd, as "monstrous kind of vermin"; the Muirs, as "gigantic insect." Politzer suggests "enormous vermin"; Sokel, "a giant kind of vermin." "Monstrous bug" is the choice of Lawson, who has written in defense of his preference.

His many legs . . . waving helplessly before his eyes

Kafkas's meticulous pseudo-Realist description produces the effect of the total reality of the metamorphosis. However absurd, its reality is never less convincing and frequently more convincing than the responses of Gregor and those around him; and yet their responses are always psychologically "true." This point is developed by Luke (28).

It was no dream

Kafka appears to stress his intention *not* to excite in the reader theories to account for the *delusion* of a metamorphosis, such as "Gregor is dreaming," "Gregor is mad," or "the entire family is mad." In bypassing the fiction of a hallucination, Kafka achieved, according to Spilka, an essential advance over the situation he borrowed from Dostoyevsky's *The Double*.

Adorno suggests that Kafka excludes the dream from his work "because everything unlike the dream and its pre-logical logic is excluded" (*Prismen*, 307). Hence the world of *The Metamorphosis* is for him dreamlike.

Greenberg's conclusion is similar. He writes: " 'It was no dream' is no contradiction of his metamorphosis' being a dream but a literal-ironical confirmation of it. Of course it is no dream—to the dreamer. The dreamer, while he is dreaming, takes his dream as real; Gregor's thought is therefore literally true to the circumstances in which he finds himself. However, it is also true ironically, since his metamorphosis is indeed no dream (meaning something unreal) but a revelation of the truth" (71).

But Hasselblatt sees an unjustified process of accomodation at work here and writes of the sentence "It was no dream": "This cannot be overheard, and therefore . . . nothing justifies enfeebling the unusual into something dreamlike" (193–94).

a little on the small side

In Weinberg's theological reading of *The Metamorphosis,* Gregor is one who claims to be the Messiah (236). Gregor's narrow room, then, "appears (forgive the somewhat brutal metaphor) on *one* level to represent quite concretely the womb of the Jewish imagination, which, it may be supposed, carries the idea of the Messiah in it but has not yet given birth to the Messiah itself and which has metamorphosed the image of Him who is generally considered to have come as the Messiah into the conception of a vermin, a monster" (257).

Sokel provides a contrasting kind of evidence. "The position of Gregor's room is, by the way, an exact duplicate of the position of Franz Kafka's room in the apartment of Herr Her[r]mann Kafka. Gregor's room is situated between his parents' and his sister's room. The members of his family communicate through the walls of his room, as if Gregor were not a human being at all or in any case not an adult, a situation which actually becomes a reality with his transformation. In the fall of 1912, when he wrote *The Metamorphosis*, Kafka's room lay between his parents' and his sister's room, as is clear from the diary entry from the period between January 7 and January 24, 1912 (T241): 'When I lay on the sofa the loud talking in the room on either side of me, by the women on the left, by the men on the right, gave me the impression that they were coarse, savage beings who could not be appeased, who did not know what they were saying . . .'" (*Franz Kafka: Tragik und Ironie*, 77; see 169).

Samsa was a traveling salesman

Landsberg notes: "When we have gone to bed the night before in unfamiliar surroundings, it is with a certain difficulty that we realize this fact as we find ourselves once more in the middle of reality [See above, note to *His many legs* . . . , 67]. This little experience occurs over and over again in the unstable life of a commercial traveler. It is not by chance that Kafka gave his hero this vocation, which like no other tends to render impossible any continuity in life" (125).

hung the picture . . . in a pretty gilt frame

Politzer notes: "[The bachelor's] hidden desires have taken refuge in his affection for this print, although the reproduction reveals in its vulgarity how deeply the standardization and commercialization of modern life had penetrated the bachelor's unconscious" (72). Adams stresses that these desires are sexual; the print is one of several clues "that [Gregor's] illness is sexual in nature. . . . A picture of impudent salacity hangs on his wall, and his only diversion has been to make with a fretsaw a frame for this pornographic fetish" (172). But Baioni surmises that this "fetish" contains an allusion to a photograph of Felice Bauer, whom Kafka had recently met and who was twice to become his fiancée.

There is no evidence from Kafka's letters to Felice that when he began writing *The Metamorphosis* on November 17, 1912, he in fact possessed a picture of her. On November 6 he wrote asking for a photograph, and on November 24 he received one, "(her) first" (F141)—a picture of Felice as a small girl! Kafka took this picture with him on the business

trip which interrupted the writing of *The Metamorphosis*
"Your picture," he wrote, "was looked at for consolation now
and again during the entire trip. Your picture lay for consolation in the night too on the chair next to my bed" (F130).
On December 3, however, Kafka received a photograph of
Felice which contains an odd allusion to the picture on
Gregor Samsa's wall. "What were you holding in your
hand?" Kafka wrote. "A strange pocketbook? And who put
those leaves in your belt? How cautiously and suspiciously,"
he continues, "you're looking at me, as if you had a slight
premonition of that tormentor who was to haunt you four
years later" (F150). The *structure* of both pictures is the
same: the woman carries a "strange" receptacle in her hand;
her middle is wrapped around with a ragged organic material;
she has assumed a defensive posture, as if to ward off the
viewer.

Nevertheless, it is useful to let Baioni's surmise stand. Together with the comments of Politzer and Adams it helps to
underscore the radical degree of irony and disparity which
marks the relation of Kafka's person and his art.

raising up against the viewer (*"dem Beschauer entgegenhob"*)

This translation of Kafka's phrase is suggested by Sokel
(*Franz Kafka: Tragik und Ironie*, 94); it captures the hostile
stance of various idolized female figures in the novels (the
Statue of Liberty in *Amerika*, the goddess of justice in *The
Trial*). In noting further the possible allusion in the picture
to Sacher-Masoch's novel *Venus in Furs*, both Sokel and
Weinberg (248) corroborate the sense of Gregor's masochism.
The usual translation of this phrase, "holding out to the
viewer," creates, on the other hand, a seductive gesture that
does not fit in easily with the woman's upright posture.

a heavy fur muff in which her whole forearm had disappeared

"From Kafka's other works," writes Kaiser, "it can be in-
ferred that for him fur is almost always the symbol of the
female genitals (as this symbol is also frequently encountered
in folklore)" (59). But this comment accurately discloses the
empty generality of psychoanalytic criticism that fuses and
dissolves the manifest textual intent into a latent biographical
intent, then confidently lends it the stature of the archetype.
It is not that the manifest biographical motive suggested by
Baioni, say, is in itself richer or more interesting than the

latent biographical motive unmasked by Kaiser. Surely the
reverse is true. But it is just because the empirical biographical intent is so insignificant in the face of Kafka's work
that its contrast with the genuine depth of the work can
be instructive.

The psychoanalytic critique, meanwhile, misleads because
of its pretensions: it considers the unconscious intent the
source and foundation of the empirical person and the work.
Thus it robs the work of its own origin, the all-metamorpho-
sing imagination. On the other hand, no one could suppose for
a moment that the origin of *The Metamorphosis* lay in any
accumulation and combination of such empirical experiences
as Kafka's snapshot of Felice Bauer, the thin walls of his
bedroom and the like. See further Kaiser (*147*).

the overcast weather . . . made him completely melancholy

And not the metamorphosis! Gregor does what he can to
resist consciousness of the terrible change. See Luke, 34ff.

which he had never felt before

On the likeness of these opening paragraphs to the opening
of Dostoyevsky's *The Double*, see Spilka, "Kafka's Sources
for *The Metamorphosis*."

For Dalmau Castañón, Gregor's "slight, dull pain" is one
of several signs pointing to a concealed symptomatology of
tuberculosis within *The Metamorphosis* (386).

"To the devil with it all"

The first of several religious "innuendos" pointed out by
Politzer (73). See below, notes to *"God Almighty"* (73) and
the bombardment with apples (89).

Pongs notes specifically: "Here the figure of speech suddenly reveals a treacherous unconscious element: the devil
is invoked. Perhaps it is really the devil who takes Gregor
at his word, the devil who, as in Thomas Mann's *Doctor
Faustus*, proves absolutely to be present by pervading with
the whole of his diabolical personality unconscious motivating
forces in the human psyche" (268).

Sokel interprets this motif further: "Immediately [after
invoking the devil, Gregor] feels an itching sensation on his
belly and touches the spot with one of his legs; but a cold
shudder ripples through him at the touch of his new body.
We note that no sooner does Gregor express the wish that the

devil free him of his job than he is reminded of his transformed body. This conjunction endows the figure of speech
with a sinister and literal significance. If we substitute
'metamorphosis' for 'devil' [in the literal formula 'The devil
take it all!'] Gregor's wish has actually been granted, for the
metamorphosis has surely taken the job from him. A parallel
to the Faust legend suggests itself, with the important quali-
fication that the 'devil's gift' to Gregor has been given him
in his sleep. At any rate Gregor has, to be sure unconsciously,
exchanged his birthright, his human form made in the image
of God, for a 'guiltless' escape from an intolerable situation.
But a chill seizes him when he realizes his new form of
existence. His shudder is the price exacted for his escape"
("Kafka's 'Metamorphosis,'" 206).

I would have quit long ago

A sign for Emrich (120) of Gregor's deep dissatisfaction
with his job and, for Sokel (174), of Gregor's basic rebellious-
ness.

talks down from the heights to the employees

Now, Schubiger observes, as a consequence of his metamorphosis Gregor will be firmly fixed into the posture of the
creeping, abased, supplicating creature (59).

Politzer sees in the figure of the boss perched on top of the
desk a reflection of the ambiguity of the economic system.
The boss sits at a distance from the employee, yet because
he is hard of hearing he requires the employee to come up
close. "The boss's personal involvement with his salesman's
family bespeaks the still patriarchal attitude of a liberal economic system when at the same time Gregor suffers from the
uniformity of life inherent in the organization methods of later
capitalism" (66–67).

on account of the boss's being hard of hearing

Benjamin notes that Kafka will not be so explicit as he is
here in "giving reasons" for the gestures which crop up in his
later works (207).

pay off my parents' debt to him

Holland sees an implicit Biblical parallel: "The description
of Gregor's boss has breadth enough to apply not just to a

petty office tyrant, but even to an Old Testament God. Indeed, the reference to the high desk echoes the Old Testament metaphor of the God 'most high' who yet can 'hear' us: 'Though the Lord be high, yet hath he respect unto the lowly' (Psalm 138:6); 'The Lord's hand is not shortened, that it cannot save; neither his ear heavy, that it cannot hear: But your iniquities have separated between you and your God, and your sins have hid his face from you, that he will not hear' (Is. 59:1–2). Read this way, the debt that Gregor assumed for his parents and must pay resembles original sin. Only after he has expiated the sin-debt can he 'take the big step' toward freedom" (145).

Weinberg also considers the parents' debts "a symbol of man's original parents and the sinfulness inherited from them" (298). See, however, the note to *The Metamorphosis* above (*63*).

Whatever the character of the parents' debt, Schubiger writes, Gregor does in fact pay it off "by embodying as a vermin everything crawling and base which in a concealed and unacknowledged way determines the behavior of the whole family" (37).

God Almighty

Pongs: "This figure of speech [literally, "Heavenly Father!"] testifies to the fact that Gregor, this average salesman, has located his average image of the world between heaven and hell. To sleep through the alarm is equal to sacrilege" (268–69).

already nearly a quarter to

Kafka's diary entry for January 16, 1922: ". . . breakdown, impossible to sleep, impossible to stay awake, impossible to endure life, or, more exactly, the course of life. The clocks are not in unison; the inner one runs crazily on at a devilish or demoniac or in any case inhuman pace, the outer one limps along at its usual speed. What else can happen but that the two worlds split apart, and they do split apart, or at least clash in a fearful manner."

Could it be that the alarm had not gone off?

Kassel notes that this sort of enacted consciousness (*erlebte Rede*) inspires in the reader a higher degree of "sympathetic

emotionality." The contrast is with the concrete sober style of
reportage bare of every emotion which dominates the rest
of the narrative (159).

He [lit., it, es] was a tool [Kreatur] of the boss

Two features of this sentence are particularly evocative.
The narrator, whose voice appears to be congruent with
Gregor's, refers to the messenger boy by means of the impersonal pronoun "it." Thus, we have an additional sign
of Gregor's staggering insensitivity to his own condition,
for it is he, of course, as vermin, who must be called "it."
Loeb formulates the point this way: Gregor's language is a
constituent of his world. Thus, an irony of fate that he
cannot know will soon humble him into the posture of a
"tool" supplicating the office manager (56).

If, on the other hand, this sentence is taken as the intrusion of a narrative voice originating at some distance from
Gregor's interior monologue, then the subject of this sentence
may well be Gregor. And this disclosure—that *Gregor* is a
tool of the boss—can stand as one of the revelations of Gregor's
life and character prior to the metamorphosis which come to
light through the mere description of his behavior after the
metamorphosis—for example, his behavior toward his sister
and toward his food.

The pronoun *es* (it), which Kafka retained throughout
all the editions of *The Metamorphosis* he prepared or helped
to prepare, is unfortunately changed without explanation to
er (he) in the collected works edited by Max Brod.

The second surprising word in this sentence is, of course,
Kreatur. This word additionally strengthens the ambiguity
about the subject of the sentence. The messenger boy may be
a "tool," but Gregor is conspicuously "the animal other than
man."

Gregor was shocked to hear his own voice

Kassel notes that the element of alienation which the
philosopher of the grotesque, Wolfgang Kayser, considers
essential to the grotesque style is evident in Gregor's fright.
Gregor's own voice seems to him someone else's, a stranger's.
It is thus fundamentally through language that Gregor grasps
his animal degradation; and so the theme of communication
emerges as the central theme of the story (160).

shuffled off

Gregor *can* therefore make himself understood when he speaks to his family. See Hasselblatt, 195–96. His father, too, appears to be satisfied by Gregor's "meticulous pronunciation"; see *10*: "even though he said this morning there wasn't [anything wrong with him]." Empson comments: ". . . if he had had the courage to go on talking he would have been less completely cut off. Here . . . is the wilful defeatism of the usual Kafka; but you can also believe that the man would have acted so within the framework of the story" (653).

feebly, but with his fist

Greenberg calls attention to the combination of weakness and strength which characterizes Mr. Samsa. Compare the line "[h]is father clenched his fist . . . ," *15*.

Within the terms of Weinberg's theological reading, in which Gregor is one who claims to be the Messiah, the father's knocking on the door with his fist is a sign of the grim future awaiting him under the shattering "fist law" of Jehovah (251).

"Do you want anything?"

Kafka's diary entry for September 15, 1912 reads: "Love between brother and sister—the repeating of the love between mother and father."

Tauber concludes: "As . . . the whole family knocks on the locked doors of Gregor's room, behind which he is hiding in the shape of a clumsy insect, the incongruousness of the demands of everyday life to this soul is revealed" (*Franz Kafka: Eine Deutung*, 27).

locking all the doors during the night, even at home

Greenberg writes: "Although he is a dutiful, self-sacrificing son, . . . he is as much a stranger to his family as he is to the world and shuts them out of his life—he locks them out as much as they lock him in" (74). See, further, Sokel (*169*).

"Just don't stay in bed being useless"

The apogee of incongruousness. See Dentan (12).

thinking things over calmly, indeed, as calmly as possible

For Hermsdorf it is "all too clear that precisely in this absurd situation neither reason nor calm reflection can help." This scene conveys "the unknowability of being" present in all of Kafka's works (96).

But "calm" ("*Ruhe*"), as Sokel points out, figures in Kafka's diaries as the sole possibility of salvation from fear and terror; see *Diaries, II*, 203 (T553). But if this calm is not to degenerate into silence, it must itself derive from the crucial factor Kafka calls "clear vision" ("*die Klarheit des Blickes*"); see *Diaries, II*, 220 (T572). Hence the next sentence—"unfortunately there was little confidence and cheer to be gotten from the view of the morning fog"—points to a disintegration of the personality. Sokel comments: "The physical condition of the metamorphosis prevents Gregor from attaining the clear vision that would hold the self together." He cannot see what is outside himself, outside his room and outside the apartment, because the metamorphosis forces a concentration of the self upon itself that endangers the existence of the person (Sokel, *Franz Kafka: Tragik und Ironie*, 302–03).

could not repress a smile

"Surely the strangest smile in world literature" (Schlingmann, 93).

Baioni instances this passage to convey the great distance from which Kafka views these proceedings. See, too, Dentan, 15ff.

almost froze, while his little legs only danced more quickly

A sign, for Schlingmann, of the radical opposition between Gregor's consciousness and Gregor's being (94).

wasn't there a single loyal dedicated worker among them

Holland notes (145): "The description of the 'firm,' with its atmosphere of universal guilt and punishment, also hints at original sin: 'A faithful man who can find?' (Prov. 20:6). Gregor and his fellow-workers are treated like the evil servant whose lord 'shall come in a day when he looketh not for him, and in an hour that he is not aware of, and shall cut him asunder, and appoint him his portion with the hypo-

crites: there shall be weeping and gnashing of teeth' (Matt.
24:50–51). Gregor is indeed cut off from men; he gets [as
will be seen] his 'portion' of garbage from his hypocritical
family, and one evening when he eavesdrops on the three
lodgers eating: 'It seemed curious to Gregor that he could hear
the gnashing of their teeth above all the clatter of cutlery'"
(145).

could one day happen even to the manager

For Schlingmann, this passage serves to implicate the reader
in Gregor's predicament—a predicament that now appears
universal rather than the destiny of an imbecile or a lower-
class worker or the member of such a family (95).

you really had to grant the possibility

Erlich links Gregor's remark with a "strikingly similar
comment" made by the narrator of Gogol's *The Nose* and
concludes: "Clearly, what is at stake here is the relevance
of the realist's favorite notion—that of verisimilitude. What
Gogol's chit-chat implicitly calls into question is the underlying assumption of realistic esthetics, namely, the belief that
social reality 'makes sense,' that human behavior yields a
discernible pattern, a stable structure of causation" (103).

the disorder of the room

"Gregor's father, before he can know of Gregor's metamorphosis, assumes that Gregor's room is untidy. He assures
his son that the chief clerk will excuse the disorder of his
room—a disorder expected of someone whom one could call
[as Gregor is afterward called] 'old dung-beetle.' Gregor's
metamorphosis into a disgusting insect seems to confirm the
father's opinion of his son" (Sokel, "Kafka's 'Metamorphosis,'"
204).

working with his fretsaw

Reiss sees in Gregor's delight in fretsaw work a sign of
his craving for creative work—a craving which his family
cannot understand (38–39).

Gregor . . . hadn't the slightest intention of letting the family down

Note the insistence with which Gregor deludes himself.

"I am speaking here in the name of your parents and of your employer"

". . . a protest against the misunderstanding with which the parent Kafkas all but crushed their strange son" (Madden, 253).

really, I practically gave my word of honor

"The grotesquely funny contradiction of the General Manager's 'truly' ["really"] and 'almost' ["practically"] reveals in one stroke that he, too, is weak-willed and oscillating" (Politzer, 67). This contrasts sharply with the qualities Sokel sees in him: "[his] arrogant tone, his readiness to suspect the worst motives, his pitiless view of an employee's decline in usefulness, so reminiscent of the Taylor 'speed-up system' . . . all these typify the inhumanity of the business from which Gregor longs to escape" ("Kafka's 'Metamorphosis,'" 207).

Sokel continues: "Whether Kafka intended to pillory the 'ethics' of the Central European business world, made merciless by the petty scale of its operations and the stiff competition, does not concern us here" (207). Adorno (*Prismen*, esp. 319ff.), Richter (*192*) and Hermsdorf (122ff.) think that such is indeed Kafka's intent.

and give my respects to the head of the firm

Luke writes: "[Gregor's] first speech . . . brilliantly crystallizes the whole atmosphere of the first chapter in its absurd aspect. It is an elaborate self-exoneration, a kaleidoscopic succession of special pleas which nullify each other, such as for example the four pairs of antithetical statements with which he begins:

"(1) He is unwell ('A slight indisposition, a dizzy spell'), but now he is well again ('But I already feel fine again').

"(2) He is still in bed, but in the act of getting out of bed.

"(3) He is still in difficulties ('I'm not as well as I thought yet') but already all is in order ('But really I'm fine').

"(4) His illness has taken him by surprise, his parents
can vouch for his having been well on the previous evening; 'or wait,' there were signs of it the
previous evening too, as his parents can attest.

"This is comic because of the implied comparison between
genuine logic and dream-logic" (37).

then Gregor had no further responsibility

Sokel sees here Gregor's desire to enjoy an "exculpated
insubordination" (174).

clinging to its slats with his little legs

For Weinberg "an obscure but . . . unmistakable figure
of the Crucifixion" (260).

Grete! Grete!

"The assonance between her name and Gregor's is indica-
tive of a deep-rooted familiarity between them" (Politzer,
71).

the voice of an animal

"Later Kafka called his own tuberculosis the 'animal'"
(Heselhaus, 362).

"Did you understand a word?" the manager was asking his parents
"That was the voice of an animal," said the manager
It was true that they no longer understood his words

Hasselblatt terms this passage unintelligible, its obscurity
due to inconsistency. For earlier the text reads, "'No,' said
Gregor. In the room on the left there was a painful silence;
. . . " And " 'Mr. Samsa,' the manager now called, . . . 'You
barricade yourself in your room, answer only "yes" and "no,"
. . . ' " " 'But, sir,' cried Gregor, beside himself . . . 'I'm
just opening up, in a minute . . .' " Hasselblatt comments:
"The contradiction is, certainly, an insignificant one; it may
have crept in while Kafka was writing hastily" (196). The
"error" is thus without meaning—a mere "manufacturer's
defect." Empson has noticed the same ambiguity concerning
Gregor's ability to communicate. "His mother," he writes,
"certainly understood one thing he said through the door

before she saw him ('there's certainly something wrong with
him, even though he said this morning there wasn't')."
Empson also considers these passages sheerly insignificant
errors, speculating that perhaps Kafka could not bear to
reread his manuscript. This surmise is incorrect.

Freedman suggests Kafka's reason for choosing to retain
these passages through successive proofreadings. They form
part of a pattern revealing the metamorphosis to be progressive. The regression of one side of Gregor Samsa to
sheer "stuff" is begun by the initial metamorphosis but entails
the successive loss of language, vision, and memory (135).

hoped for marvelous, amazing feats from both the doctor and the locksmith

Greenberg notes that sending for the doctor is the mother's
suggestion, for she considers the metamorphosis to be an
illness; and sending for the locksmith, the father's: he considers his son a nuisance, bent on causing him annoyance.
Thus Gregor "agrees with both parents, unable to distinguish
between the element of recalcitrance and refusal and the
element of illness in his withdrawal into inhuman isolation"
(77).

turning the key in the lock with his mouth

Thus Gregor is just big enough, when standing upright,
to touch the keyhole. In the course of comparing *David
Copperfield* with *The Metamorphosis* Spilka furnishes this
Freudian comment: "Both prisoners use the keyhole to gain
access to parental figures; . . . both use it in a sensual manner, and Gregor even bites down upon a key (the sign of
masculine authority) . . ." (302).

a brown liquid . . . dripped onto the floor

How foreign must Gregor's body be for him, and how much
a mere instrument, if he has to *infer* from "a" liquid that he is
hurting himself in some way (Schubiger, 63).

He first had to edge slowly

"The moment Gregor opens the door and shows himself
in his new shape to the chief clerk, the roles of the two are
reversed in fact, even though Gregor does not recognize this.
The chief clerk, who has come to threaten Gregor, now

retreats in terror while Gregor, hitherto the poor exploited and despised salesman, drives him out of the apartment so that he leaves his hat and cane behind, tokens of Gregor's triumph" (Sokel, "Kafka's 'Metamorphosis,' " 208).

when he heard the manager burst out with a loud "Oh!"

Binion (215) considers the manager's exclamation and the reaction of Gregor's parents as a sign of their instantly recognizing him—hence, part of the proof that the metamorphosis is in fact only a delusion on the part of the sick hero.

with heaves of his powerful chest

Benjamin notes that this is the typical posture, too, of the authority figure Klamm of *The Castle* when he is alone, and the posture depicted in the portrait of the castellan: "his head bowed so deeply on his chest that his eyes are hardly visible" (197). Greenberg observes that this combination of fierceness and helplessness characterizes Mr. Samsa throughout *The Metamorphosis*.

it was a hospital

Another image strengthening the connection between the metamorphosis and the onset of a severe illness. See von Wiese, 330.

in large, separately visible drops

This device of freezing time is reminiscent of Kafka's earlier prose experiments, for example "Wedding Preparations in the Country": "Now and then there came men who were smoking, bearing small upright elongated clouds along ahead of them" (*Dearest Father*, 2).

reading various newspapers

An indirect criticism of Gregor's father, notes Binder—at least from Gregor's point of view. Gregor had protested against those other salesmen who, like harem women, eat late-morning breakfasts (353).

respect for his bearing and his rank

Photographs, particularly old and faded photographs, recur in Kafka's work, furnishing the shock of *déjà vu*. The immortalized gesture, the frozen instant, reflect eloquently and frequently terribly a dimension "beneath individuation." See Adorno, *Prismen*, 313–14.

Margolis' comment ascribes to the picture a similar function: If this photograph is not to be a happy coincidence, it must reflect (in the Platonic perspective) the domination over Gregor's reason of the appetitive and aggressive element of his nature (36).

For Ulshöfer the picture reflects Gregor's alienated social identity: "Kafka means to say that the family shows Gregor respect for his social position as a lieutenant; but it is the uniform which is the source of the lieutenant's bearing. The family sees its pride and dignity symbolically represented in this photograph" (29).

Loeb develops this point: the picture constitutes a metamorphosis; it covers up the unsuspected reality of Gregor's odium. For this reason it is like the superficial appearance of Mr. Samsa at the close of Part II and in Part III; his uniform covers up the insectlike existence of a parasitic senility— but soon enough shows the stains of everyday reality. The uniform is the outward expression of a self-alienation (53). See below, note to *his official uniform even in the house, 91.*

suffer on his own person the grim consequences

Goldstein observes that, beyond psychosomatically linking Gregor's emotional and bodily pain, this passage suggests an interpretation of the metamorphosis: "that with his transformation and the progressively severe inflictions, Gregor suffers macrocosmically all that which he had experienced, in a small and limited way, throughout his adult years" (209). This idea, however, overlooks the fact that Gregor's metamorphosis enables him to experience new modes of pleasure as well.

I'm at least partly right

Politzer sees in Gregor's speech an excellent example of the salesman's rhetoric; unfortunately, Gregor is unaware that he is no longer selling fabrics—but himself. For Schubiger, Gregor's rhetoric exactly apes the style and language of the office manager's previous speech to him. Luke observes: "The second of Gregor's two speeches . . . is virtually his last attempt to make himself understood verbally, and occurs at the moment when the others see him for the first time;

thus the horrific effect here tends to overlay the comedy of
the speech, which is also full of ironies so extreme that
Gregor himself seems to be sadistically conscious of them"
(37).

as if awaiting him there

Pongs observes: "The linguistic forms of the 'as if' with
which Gregor's shock effect on the manager is depicted do
not stem from Gregor's perspective but from the writer, who
knows himself to be in the devil's pay" (281).

unearthly [transcendental] deliverance

"From the climax, the 'longing for transcendental deliverance,' we grasp that the sight of the gigantic cockroach has
struck the manager as a manifestation of Satan. The satanic
drives forth the longing for the transcendental in the rational
businessman" (Pongs, 269).

But his sister was not there

Edel underscores the fact that while it dawns on Gregor
that he is cut off from all the others, while he loses his economic mainstay and is immured in his room by his father, his
sister is in flight, even if in search of help—to be sure, from
strangers (222).

final recovery from all his sufferings was imminent

Schlingmann stresses that Gregor's hope arises under the
influence of his verminous condition, which now gives him a
moment of joy. The final recovery he contemplates evidently
points to a reverse metamorphosis into Gregor Samsa, son and
salesman, but would this really constitute a final release from
all his suffering? (96) By way of a reply, Greenberg writes:
"With supreme illogic he derives a hope of release from his
animal condition from the very comfort he gets by adapting
himself to that condition—so divided is his self-consciousness
from his true self. But there is a second meaning, which piles
irony upon the irony: precisely as a noisome outcast from the
human world Gregor feels the possibility of relief, of final
relief. Only as an outcast does he sense the possibility of an
ultimate salvation rather than just a restoration of the status
quo" (80).

"Help, for God's sake, help!"

According to Pongs, the mother cries as if she too were beseeching God for his help against a satanic apparition.

he could not resist snapping his jaws

Moments before, when Gregor was biting on the key, a brown liquid came gushing from these same wounded jaws. Thus a parallel arises between the bodily traumas suffered by Gregor and the actual damages and degradations of his environment—the link being Gregor's involuntary sense of responsibility and anguish for these damages.

Sokel sees Gregor's gesture as revealing to his family the aggressiveness of which Gregor himself is ignorant (175).

the manager . . . leaped down several steps and disappeared;

Schubiger notes that it take five pages for the office manager to reach the bottom of the staircase; these five pages are devoted to Gregor's speeches and reflections. "Either with the flight of the office manager we are to imagine an extremely slow, stylized movement, more or less like those in Expressionist films, or we are to assume that time for Gregor is different from what it is for the others" (35). This moment may also be seen as an expression of Kafka's striving to overtake reality, which always has, as it were, a head start on the self. But the gap is unbridgeable; the self delays; and we are forever in default.

hissing like a wild man

Within the terms of Weinberg's theological reading, "the hissing sounds of the raging father quite possibly attempt to remind the son of the *snake of Paradise*, of unatoned and very likely inextinguishable original sin" (272).

For the Jungian psychoanalyst Webster, "The father image hisses with the noise of many snakes and seems to be the force driving the beetle back into the symbolic womb." In fact, however, the seduction of the womb arises from the sexual field between *mother* and son; "the serpent who tempts the woman to sin is but a projection of a man's own inhibited sexuality" (352). See 158.

like [the voice] of only a single father

For Hillman this is an instance of a decisive moment at which descriptive significance passes into symbolic significance; here "the father, who until now has been shown as a very bourgeois, comfortable figure, even if a rather dangerous one when his comfort is disturbed, suddenly undergoes an enlargement and superelevation, which makes him appear as an almost mythic prosecuting body bent on annihilation" (139).

The door was slammed shut with the cane

Adorno notes a similar gesture in *The Trial*, when Josef K. glimpses for a moment the repetition of an event from the preceding day—his warders are being beaten—and then "'slam[s] the door shut and beat[s] on it with his fists as if that would shut it more securely.' This is the gesture of Kafka's own work, which from time to time, like that of Poe's, turns away from the most extreme scenes, as if no eye could survive the sight" (*Prismen*, 314).

at last everything was quiet

After the agonizing blow dealt Gregor, "as though nothing further could be imagined or significant, the caesura between the parts of the story provides the kind of silence, comparable to a gasp of horror and astonishment, which the reader needs before he can continue" (Goldstein, 208).

he didn't like the milk at all

In terms of Weinberg's theological reading: "Here once again Gregor's exclusion from Jewry is underscored: he no longer finds to his taste the *kosher*, 'suitable,' food of the ritual cookery which [the milk and white bread] appear to represent, their symbolic white color vouching for their purity" (276).

had recently been discontinued altogether

See below, note to *spread out on an old newspaper, 86*.

86 THE METAMORPHOSIS

were to come to a horrible end?

In Luke's view, here Gregor "rises to the most advanced level of thought shown by any character throughout the story" (31).

she brought him a wide assortment

Grete's solicitude has the effect of confirming Gregor's animal identity.

spread out on an old newspaper

Sparks shows that the newspaper is a highly charged image in this work: it is a "ceremonial property"; the person in power at any moment possesses or manipulates it. Thus before the metamorphosis Gregor used to like to sit at the table and read the newspaper; immediately after the metamorphosis we learn that the father drags out breakfast by reading various newspapers. The father has driven Gregor back into his room with a huge newspaper (78).

his bruises must have completely healed

Greenberg notes: "The vitality possible to him in his pariah state (if he can only find the food he needs to feed his spiritual hunger on, for he is 'unusually hungry') is in sharp contrast with his human debility" (80).

That immediately startled [shocked] him (schreckte ihn auf)

Kafka's letters to Felice show how frequently Kafka was shocked. He writes, for example, on November 26, 1912: "I have never since, I think, been so horrified as the time you found a strange tone in my letter, but other little remarks shock me enough as it is. I'm shocked to read that your mother wants to protect you against any disappointment, when I read about your acquaintance from Breslau . . . ; I'm shocked to hear that you love me, and if I were not to hear it I'd want to die" (F129).

his parents and the maid were still asleep

Ruth Hein suggests, very plausibly, that this maid is a new maid, a young girl of sixteen (32), come to replace Anna (9, 13), the former maid. Aware, on the day of Gregor's metamorphosis, of something sinister in the house, Anna has obtained permission to leave (26). Because Anna also used to do the cooking, she is sometimes referred to as the cook (32).

they were suffering enough as it was

"Through all this," notes Weinberg, "complete incommunicability reigns" (280).

"He's left everything again."

Fresh evidence for the view of an ongoing metamorphosis.

the collapse of his business five years before

"After the collapse of Gregor's father's business, Gregor's boss became his father's creditor. Thus the two firms were financially connected, and the father's position must also have had an effect on Gregor's career. During the earlier period Gregor was only a stock clerk" (Binder, 354).

regardless of the great expense involved

"Gregor was no friend of music. He weighed its value in cash, and he may have desired to incur this 'great expense' partly out of spite, because the parents would have opposed it. There was a first faint sign of rebellion hidden behind this idea, for the rest of his earlier history as a man was completely free of the desire for anything subtler than the fur lady on his print" (Politzer, 76–77).

Often he lay the whole night through

Kafka said to Janouch: "Perhaps my insomnia only conceals a great fear of death. Perhaps I am afraid that the soul —which in sleep leaves me—will not be able to return. Perhaps insomnia is only an all-too-vivid sense of sin, which is afraid of the possibility of a sudden judgment. Perhaps insomnia is itself a sin. Perhaps it is a rejection of the natural" (Janouch, *Gespräche*, 194–95). And elsewhere: "If there were not these ghastly sleepless nights, I would not write at all. But in this way I am always conscious of my dark solitary confinement" (Janouch, *Gespräche*, 32).

evidently in some sort of remembrance

If Kafka wished to stress the mediated and detached character of Gregor's experience of others by adopting almost continually throughout the story the perspective of Gregor, here Kafka compounds the theme by himself adopting a mediated and detached relation to Gregor (Schubiger, 71).

less and less distinctly

Further evidence for the view of an ongoing metamorphosis.

he was now completely covered up

Gregor the "untouchable" is now "invisible" as well. See Schubiger, 39.

almost happy absent-mindedness

See 105.

only his mother's voice, which he had not heard for so long

This detail, Empson notes, is "quite incompatible with the previous story" (653). Gregor has heard his mother crying, "Let me go to Gregor, he is my unfortunate boy!" And yet Kafka's point is clear: for a long time Gregor has not heard his mother speak of him with such directness and concern. The overpowering force of his forgetfulness is linked to the absence of love.

and soothed his hot belly

Politzer writes: "The insect sits on the picture as if he were possessing the woman in it. Gregor is at the same time united with the picture of the fur lady and separated from his dream object by the glass. The fulfillment and simultaneous frustration of love are rendered here by a convincing paradox" (72).

with raised fist

The gesture of the balled fist appears in the coat of arms of Kafka's native city, Prague (Weinberg, 291).

with a scrupulously exact, gleaming part

Richter notes: "To refute the supposition that a genuine power had perhaps been present in Gregor and that [as a wage earner] he could have performed a necessary function—and thus to prove the complete truth of the degrading metamorphosis—Kafka introduces a positive transformation in the life of the family paralleling Gregor's gradual decline" (115).

with a sullen look on his face

Now it is the father who in his uniform "demands respect for his bearing and his rank" (Binder, 354).

the gigantic size of the soles of his boots

"What becomes of a man who is a bug as big as a human being? As big as adults must appear to the child, and as distorted, with gigantic, trampling legs and far-off, tiny heads, were one to catch and isolate the child's terrified vision; it could be photographed with an oblique camera" (Adorno, *Prismen*, 317).

he had not had very reliable lungs

Biographical critics, such as Dalmau Castañón (387) and Heselhaus (362), see in this detail an allusion to Kafka's incipient tuberculosis.

his father was determined to bombard him

"These apples are . . . related to the Tree in the Garden of Eden, Paradise Lost, love, cognition, and sin" (Politzer, 73). Schlingmann adds: "The apple scene appears as an inversion of the Fall: Gregor does not himself reach out for the fruit; it is thrown at him, rather, as punishment for his regression to a prehuman stage" (101). "But," writes Schubiger, "the reader concerned with the foreground of the action and not its metaphysical background will see in the father's gesture a naturalness and matter-of-factness suited to his character. In his battle with his son the father seizes at random the article nearest at hand, while Gregor remains tangled in fine speculations" (46). "These weapons [these apples], literally so trivial and symbolically so heavy, crash upon Gregor with the full weight of his father's once-successful and now regained sensuality" (Adams, 174).

The apples' being red presumably means that they are soft. Empson sees this point as involving Kafka in a minor inconsistency. If Gregor's back is "as hard as armor plate," and if "nothing was likely to happen to it when it fell on the carpet," how then could the apple crack this carapace and make it fester?" "No doubt it is the apple of Adam, but one wants the details more convincing"(653).

This objection disappears, of course, if the vulnerability of Gregor's carapace is considered a further sign of his debilitation.

literally forced its way into Gregor's back

"Literally" translates "*förmlich*" but misses the pun. "*Förmlich*" can mean "literally, absolutely" but also "formally, *pro forma*." It is thus another instance of ambiguity tending to confirm Beissner's and Binion's hypothesis that the metamorphosis is only a hallucination.

complete confusion of all his senses

See Kaiser, 155.

but now Gregor's sight went dim

This failure of sight marks the onset of unconsciousness. But it should not come as a complete surprise to the reader; it is as much a sudden catastrophe as an intense moment of the progressive sensory degeneration already indicated. See above, note to *less and less distinctly*, 88.

begged for Gregor's life

"As the door separates Gregor from his kind, so too in this novella fainting, the shutting off of the body from consciousness, separates Gregor from the possibly comforting sight of his mother pleading with his father to spare his life, a sight that would perhaps have affected him as a proof of maternal solicitude and love" (Sonnenfeld, 224). Sonnenfeld is, however, the only one of Kafka's critics to neglect the traumatic character of this "primal scene," to use Freud's term. See, for example, Kaiser, *154*.

Binion, who holds that the metamorphosis is Gregor's hallucination, writes: "The presentation of the scene according to Gregor's mode of perception brings out the affective basis for his shock. The rhythmic pursuit of Gregor by the father, agitated and erect in his uniform, followed by Gregor's slow passage through a double door back into his dark chamber, the father loading his pockets with apples and then discharging them while the mother, giddy, disrobed, 'embrac[es] him, in complete union with him— . . .' —the scene requires only an instant's elaboration by Gregor to become a fantasy of his own procreation, hostile and violent. Presumably it revives in him a like pseudomemory at the root of his illness. Schizophrenics have fantasies of the sort often enough without the benefit of provocation, so strong in them is the urge to undo their birth and conception. Obedient to this urge Gregor reverts to primary narcissism, simulates embryonic life in the sickroom, and finally curls up and dies" (218).

Adorno points out that this sort of preoccupation with the events with which psychoanalysis is concerned links Kafka and Freud in the specific sense that both conceive these events as actual and not as subjective delusions or inventions (*Prismen*, 310–12).

In *Psychosexueller Infantalismus* Stekel comments: "Metamorphosis into a little animal for the purpose of sexual observation also plays an important role in the mental life of children. Children want to be a fly or a flea in order to investigate the secrets of the bedroom without being recognized. The fairy tale also takes into account this form of zoöanthropical fantasy" (263).

the living room door . . . was opened

"Considering how much [Gregor] is supposed to stink, it is unlikely that they would take to leaving his door open in the evening so that he can watch them; but perhaps this shows how remorseful his father was for throwing the apple" (Empson, 653).

The open door fulfills a function for the perspective governing the story. "Kept ajar, it enables Gregor (like the reader) to be simultaneously in two different places" (Sonnenfeld, 224).

to take off his official uniform even in the house

"Significantly, the father keeps wearing his uniform even at home. Of course it gets soiled in the process, and his life is thus involuntarily brought into relation to Gregor's disgusting being. The secret unconquerableness of the disorder, the depths into which Gregor is sinking, is revealed" (Tauber, *Franz Kafka: Eine Deutung*, 30). See above, note to *he could not resist snapping his jaws*, 84.

all the mother's and sister's care

"The world of order carried into the home destroys the possibility of true human love" (Taylor, 338).

"Look at that old dung beetle [Mistkäfer]!"

In "Kafka's 'Metamorphosis,'" Sokel writes: "*Mistkäfer* literally means any species of beetle whose habitat is dung, garbage, and dirt generally. According to Meyer's *Lexikon* the term includes three subgroups of the beetle—aphodinae, coprinae, and geotrupinae. The translation given in Cassell's and Herbert's German-English dictionaries is 'dung-beetle.' Mr. Lloyd in his translation of the story uses the term 'cockroach,' which comes closer than the Muir 'dung-beetle' to Kafka's meaning, since Gregor lives not in a farmyard, but in a city apartment" (203, n. 4).

Freedman would insist on keeping the term "dung beetle" precisely because it is a country bug, not a city vermin. Kafka's own father, an ambitious self-made businessman, settled as a young man in Prague after a harsh boyhood in the wretched provincial village of Wossek. If Herr Samsa is linked to Kafka's father, then his horror cannot be greater than to have his scion and support transformed into a gross image of his own rural beginnings.

Holland notes that beetles, unlike cockroaches, undergo total metamorphosis. Further, dung beetles are scarabs. The Egyptians venerated the scarab as an image of the sacred dung beetle linked to the sun god. Samson (Samsa) means in Hebrew "the sun's man." The German word for the title of the story, *Die Verwandlung*, means not only insect metamorphosis and transformation in general, but also transsubstantiation (see above note to *The Metamorphosis* (*Die Verwandlung*), 63). "The dung-beetle, then," Holland concludes, "was the one animal that gave Kafka everything he needed: total metamorphosis from a wingless grub to a hard-working, traveling-salesman-like adult plus the combination of lothesomeness and divinity" (149).

Politzer maintains a contrary position. He declares that "when the charwoman finally calls [Gregor] 'an old dung beetle' she does not, as one critic [Sokel] maintains, pronounce an entomological classification, but simply adds an insult to Gregor's fatal injury" (81).

Spilka develops this point differently. The charwoman's words, he writes, stress transcendent life: "They are couched as a friendly insult [see *Diaries, II*, 104]; they give a name to his affliction, they include and absorb deformity through acceptance, and so accentuate his human worth." Gregor is in error to answer her friendly insult with indignation and annoyance. This is, after all, "the first time in the story another human being has been willing to accept him" (*Dickens and Kafka*, 78–79).

three roomers

Since these roomers regularly have breakfast and sometimes have their evening meal at the Samsas, I refer to them as "boarders" in sentences where the word "roomer" would be infelicitous. Kafka always refers to them by the same word—"*Zimmerherr*." [S.C.]

Baioni sees these figures as a prefiguration of that world of bourgeois functionaries which comes into its own in *The Trial* (100).

Sparks works out in considerable detail the thesis that the story of the three roomers recapitulates Gregor's metamorphosis. Together the roomers constitute an uncanny being, no less burdensome for the Samsas or importunate than Gregor himself. Like Gregor in the old days, they usurp the father's position at the table; like Gregor both before and after his metamorphosis, they move in insect-like synchronization.

Whatever was not being used at the moment was just flung into Gregor's room

Schubiger sees in this detail the suggestion that Gregor's verminous existence illustrates the true nature of the Samsa family. They lay their own nullity, so to speak, at Gregor's door. Thus Gregor's life exhibits what the others out of weakness refuse to recognize in their own lives (39).

to examine (prüfen) them before eating

For Sparks "a direct literal allusion to Gregor's sampling the dishes put in front of him at the beginning of the second part" (78)—one of several signs that point unequivocally to the identification of Gregor with the roomers.

they read and smoked

The roomers have gained preeminence over the Samsas in their own house. This fact is shown by their dominating the dining table and reading the newspaper.

his indifference to everything

More than his "indifference" surely; there is the apple festering in his back. (This inconsistency is noted by Empson, 653.) It appears to be part of Kafka's strategy to mute through irony Gregor's ecstatic privileged moment to follow.

paid any attention to him

"To show oneself is in the end to appeal to the humanity of the others, to remind them of the task of liberation which must be accomplished jointly. But Gregor's heedless display of his wretchedness also leads to nothing" (Edel, 224).

his sister was playing so beautifully

This is the first manifestation in Gregor of a sense of beauty; as a human being, he did not love music (Sonnenfeld, 223).

that music could move him so

Von Wiese notes: "This important passage is by no means unambiguous. It can mean: Even if the whole world considers me an animal, I am still not one, because only human beings can be so moved by music. But it can also be interpreted to mean the exact opposite: Gregor, about whom we learned earlier that he did not have so intimate a relation to music as his sister, now obtains it on the primitive-emotional basis of his animal organization and in so doing becomes more clearly conscious of being an animal as well" (328).

On the grounds of this second interpretation, Greenberg accuses Gregor of once again failing "to grasp the positive possibility contained in the truth about himself and his death in life—the possibility of . . . spiritual life through outcastness" (82). The way Gregor interprets the experience of music is clearly an error. "It is nonsensical to associate music and bestiality, music is at the opposite pole from bestiality. His metamorphosis is a path to the spiritual rather than the bestial" (82).

But Luke finally maintains the absolute ambiguity of the

passage by giving a positive value to Gregor's association of music and "bestiality." He writes: "Has he become less, or more than human—merely infantile, or mature in a different dimension of maturity? Or is not illness a kind of holiness, and anguished primitive fantasy the substance of art and religion, and may not the energy of savage instinct serve the loftiest aims?" (40).

were coming to light

In the preceding sentence, von Wiese writes, Kafka blurs the distinction between animal and human; but in doing so he creates a transition leading to the "unknown nourishment" which itself lies beyond the antithesis between man and animal and points to some mystic sphere. At the outset Gregor rejected the food offered him because it was insufficiently substantial and suited only for an animal. Now the opposite is the case: Gregor longs for less-material food.

"Here," writes Hillman, "Kafka unambiguously goes beyond the realistic plane. . . . That Gregor longs for any kind of unknown nourishment is at this juncture news to the reader. But now suddenly the text speaks not only of any kind of nourishment, but of *the* longed-for nourishment. And it is of course obvious that we are dealing here, not with concrete, real nourishment, but with music. But music, too, is not meant as aesthetic and acoustic spiritual enjoyment. On the contrary, it only refers to another music, a sphere lying beyond it to which it first shows the way. . . . In the hypothetical locution an image breaks through which may be described as existential since music, like 'ground' and 'food,' always indicates in Kafka being itself" (139).

Anders comments on Kafka's significant usage of the subjunctive, as in this passage. If the mania for interpretation which possesses Kafka's characters is the result of their powerlessness to govern and change things, it is also an essentially poetic faculty, projecting possibilities and irrealities. "From the smallest springboard of reality Kafka's figures leap into the wide and tangled horizons of the 'ifs' and the subjunctive . . ." (49). See also Schubiger, 95ff.

Christmas had certainly come and gone?

Weinberg—for whom Gregor's metamorphosis figures as a noble parody of Messianic passion—writes: "However, instead of experiencing the fulfillment of these beautiful dreams for the future [of union with the sister, 'the daughter of Zion, the new Jerusalem, the bride of Christ'], Gregor has to note that with 'Christmas come and gone' the precondition of such hopes went by unused" (304).

Politzer's view is different. "Even here in this feverish wish dream, [Gregor] feels compelled to make sure that Christmas is long past, as if with its passing his obligation also has been abolished. He not only wants to possess what cannot be possessed, but also refuses to pay for it" (77).

kiss her on the neck

In a world without metamorphosis, writes von Wiese, Gregor's display of affection, despite its intensity, would still have been acceptable. The fact that here it is so terrifying and grotesque is a tribute to Kafka's imagination: for "in the meantime the reader has grown accustomed . . . to the fact fictively introduced that Gregor has become, irrevocably, a monstrous, disgusting bug" (341).

Dentan notes further: "Of course, this last remark ["kiss her on the neck"], one will say, has its natural place and meaning in the horrible necessity of the story; but it is so unexpected and despite its logic so absurd that one divines behind it a playful (ludique) intention of the author" (13).

Kafka's playfulness throughout this piece is a dimension of the greatest significance. For Dentan it is chiefly a guarantee of aesthetic distance from Gregor and his plight, maintained by the narrator and communicated to the reader; for Spilka this distance is proof of a transcendent humanity (see above note to "Look at that old dung beetle!" 92). Kafka's irony refutes Beissner's notion that the immanent perspective of the story makes of it the immediate representation of Kafka's "dream-like inner life" (See Henel, 252).

without a ribbon [Band] or collar

In the course of his interpretation of the religious symbolism of The Metamorphosis Weinberg comments: "Thus the sister with her [bare] neck—'free,' unbound, 'without a ribbon (it is redeemed from the bond * of the old covenant [Bund], from the Jewish religio) represents in Gregor's imagination the exact opposite of the lady with the fur boa cut out from

---

* The German word das Band can mean "ribbon," "band," or "bond."

the illustrated newspaper—whose image Gregor was trying to protect just a short time ago" (304).

Schlingmann, on the other hand, stresses not the difference but the similarity between these two erotic daydreams. He writes: "Here Gregor conjures up an idyll for himself which allows him as a vermin to lead a parasitical existence; in this way he can avoid giving himself to a woman he does not know without having to renounce his cravings for possession" (98).

the middle roomer first smiled at his friends

Another sign, for Binion (215), that Gregor is not a vermin but a neurotic who thinks he is one.

then looked at Gregor again

No fulfillment, as Greenberg points out, has come to Gregor Samsa as a result of his excursion; the living room, "with the three indignant lodgers staring down at him, is the same old public world of bullying businessmen he knew as a traveling salesman" (82).

"We too give notice as of now"

Dentan notes that the symmetrical movements of the three roomers suggest the mechanical movements of puppets and makes ludicrous their lofty and reproving tone. The effect is similar to the puncturing of the pretentions of the office manager in Section I. Both effects tend to heighten the reader's sense of his own distance from, and domination of, this horrible situation (12).

In this matter Adorno remarks (concerning the frozen immortalized gesture, which recurs in Kafka and produces the terrible shock of the *déjà vu*): "The sameness or intriguing similarity of a plurality [of things] ranks among Kafka's most stubborn motifs; all possible half-creatures step up in pairs, frequently with the stamp of the childish or silly, oscillating between good nature and cruelty like savages in children's books. Individuation has become such a burden for men, and has remained so precarious up to the present, that they are frightened to death whenever its veil lifts a little" (*Prismen*, 315).

The point is that those pairs (or triplets) in *The Metamorphosis* objectify the terror of the experience of the *déjà vu* which threatens the individual identity.

this monster [Untier]

"Monster" translates the German "*Untier*," of which Pongs notes: "the figure of the bug remains in the uncanny condition of the 'un'" (279). See above, note to *monstrous vermin (ungeheueres Ungeziefer)*, 66.

he would have gone away of his own free will

Schlingmann detects the contradiction in Grete's argument: Gregor could leave voluntarily only if he were at once an animal and not an animal, if he had Gregor's insight but at the same time weren't Gregor but only a monster (99).

without realizing it

"Only the way [to a fulfillment of being] can be represented and in it the intention to experience that moment—in other words, only the endless searching of Kafka's figures after the possibility of freedom outside the compulsion of the way. From this it follows that time changes with respect to measurable clock time; the spatial distance covered corresponds to the quality of the events, as changing time. And so it comes about that one and the same distance can now be shorter, now longer, according to the intensity with which it has been traversed" (von Brück, 120).

Taylor notes specifically: "The reader knows the reason—he had been receiving the unknown nourishment that he craved" (341).

even firmer than his sister's

Kafka wrote in "Reflections on Sin, Suffering, Hope and the True Way": "A first sign of the beginnings of awareness is the wish to die" (H40, aphorism 13).

three in the morning

Sparks detects "once again the magic 'three' which is to be regarded as the ritual number of the novella" (80). See also Adams, 173.

His conviction that he would have to disappear . . . streamed his last weak breath

Holland notes that "the account of Gregor's death parallels the Biblical accounts of Christ's death: 'Now from the sixth

hour there was darkness over all the land unto the ninth hour'
(Matthew 27:45). 'After this, Jesus knowing that all things
were accomplished that the scripture might be fulfilled . . .
said, It is finished: and He bowed His head, and gave up the
ghost' (John 19:28–30)" (147).

anywhere in the apartment

Holland notes this further Biblical parallel: " 'Behold, the
veil of the temple was rent in twain from the top to the bottom; and the earth did quake, and rocks rent; and the graves
were opened; and many bodies of the saints which slept
arose' (Matthew 27:51–52)" (148).

the long broom

For Sparks the broom, in being passed from Grete to the
cleaning woman, becomes in the course of the action a
"clearly ambiguous, ceremonial, keeper's instrument": it keeps
Gregor at a distance and is used to take care of his room
(75). See above note, to *spread out on an old newspaper*, 86.

The couple Mr. and Mrs. Samsa

The transformation of father and mother into Mr. and Mrs.
Samsa is an external sign of the shift in narrative perspective–a shift in the direction of banality and smug petit-bourgeois optimism (Schlingmann, 89).

Mrs. Samsa

"For the rest of the story she appears more and more as
her husband's appendage; literally Gregor's mother becomes
more and more a Mrs. Samsa" (Politzer, 69).

He crossed himself

"With the sign of the cross one keeps the devil—as well as
a devastating insight—at a distance" (Schubiger, 53).

went hopping right after him

The German word *hüpfen* (to hop) underscores the insect-
like character of this movement, for *Hüpfer* is a familiar dialectical word for "grasshopper."

then up on past them

Weinberg sees in this figure a symbol, marked by bitter humor, of Gregor's ascension, of the resurrection of the flesh (241).

Holland amplifies: "Priest-like, he brings the meat that the Samsas will eat themselves, suggesting communion, as opposed to the burnt offerings they had formerly made to the lodgers" (150).

three letters of excuse

"Gregor cannot communicate either truths or falsehoods. . . . On the other hand, the family readily seizes an occasion to falsify excuses for their absence from work. . . . The implication is that the commercial world has anticipated and accommodated minor lapses at least for some of its creatures" (Margolis, 40).

to find her a good husband

Ruth Hein perceives here the story's "rather terrifying realization that having exploited (dehumanized) their son, the Samsas will now do the job on the daughter."

their daughter got up (erhob sich)

The Muirs translate this phrase as "their daughter sprang to her feet," thus concluding the account of the family's recovery on an emphatic note of vitality. The Muirs' interpretation of this sentence has inspired critics to draw a parallel between the conclusion of "A Hunger Artist" and *The Metamorphosis* on the basis of the parallel between the vital movements (of the leopard and of Grete) at the close of both stories. But the tonality of the conclusion of *The Metamorphosis* in fact opposes this idea; the story ends on a palpably subdued and melancholy note, which must be kept in translation. See Kafka's *Briefe an Felice*, 163.

stretched her young body.

"Kafka was no longer satisfied with this ending while correcting the story on January 19, 1914" (Heselhaus, 362). See *112*. It is not certain, of course, just how much of the story Kafka considers its "ending."

In Greenberg's view, the narrative form of *The Metamor-*

phosis is radically non-Aristotelian: it has its climax at the beginning and no dénouement or conclusion (69–70). Politzer sees in it something like an analytical tragedy, for it "shows but the last stages of the hero's ordeal; yet the crucial element of analytic dramaturgy—the posing of the guilt question and the gradual discovery of its answer—is neglected here" (65). Luke, on the other hand, sees in *The Metamorphosis* a classically balanced "dramatic pattern of exposition, conflict and dénouement" (29).

DOCUMENTS

Letter by Kafka to Max Brod,
October 8, 1912

After some good writing in the night from Sunday to Monday—I could have gone on writing all through the night, and all day, and all night and all day, and finally flown away—and today I am sure I could have written well, too—one page, really only the last dying breath of yesterday's ten, is even finished, I must stop for the following reason: Mr. X, the factory owner, early this morning went away on business, which I, in my fond absent-mindedness, hardly noticed, and will be off for ten or fourteen days. While he is away the factory is really left in control of the works manager alone, and no employer, least of all one so anxious as my father, will doubt that the most utter fraud is now being perpetrated in the factory. I myself in fact believe it too, although not so much for the sake of the money, but because of my ignorance and pangs of conscience. But after all, even an impartial person, so far as I can imagine such a person, couldn't have very much doubt that my father's fears are justified, even though I must not forget that I myself, at bottom, cannot comprehend why a German works manager from Germany, even during the absence of Mr. X, whose superior he is by far in every technical and organizing question, should not be able to keep everything running in the same good order as usual; for after all, we are men, not thieves. . . .

When I was trying to tell you some time ago that nothing from outside can disturb me when I am writing (which was said, of course, not as a boast, but to comfort myself), I was only just thinking how my mother whimpers to me almost every evening, that I should

after all take a look at the factory now and again just
to keep father's mind easy, and how father has said the
same thing, on his side, in a far nastier way with looks
and in other indirect ways. All this whimpering at me
and reproaching me wouldn't, for the most part, amount
to stupidity were it not that—and that, one can't deny
it for all the world, is where the stupidity of all this talk
lies—I can't bear such a control even in my brightest
moments.

But it's not a question of that for the next fortnight,
when all that is necessary is that any pair of eyes, even
mine, should wander about over the factory. I can't make
the slightest objection to this demand being made of me,
of all people, because everybody thinks that I am chiefly
responsible for founding the factory—though I must have
taken this responsibility on in a dream, it seems to me at
least—and moreover, there is no one here besides me
who can go to the factory, because my father and mother,
of whose going one couldn't dream, anyhow, are now
in the middle of their busiest season (business seems to
be going better in the new shop, too) and today, for
example, mother didn't even come home for lunch.

So when mother once more began the same old story
this evening, and, apart from the reference to making my
father unhappy and ill by my behavior, produced the
further reason of Mr. X's business journey and the complete desertion of the factory, a wave of bitterness—I
don't know if it was only gall—passed through my whole
body, I saw perfectly that I had only the alternatives of
either waiting until everyone had gone to bed and then
jumping out of the window, or of going every day to the
factory and sitting in X's office every day for the next
fourteen days. The former would have given me the opportunity of rejecting all responsibility both for inter-
rupting my writing and for deserting the factory, the
latter would have interrupted my writing without any
doubt—I can't just rub fourteen nights' sleep out of my
eyes—and would leave me, if I had enough strength of
will and hope, the prospect of perhaps being able to
begin again where I stopped today, fourteen days later.

So I didn't jump out through the window, and also the temptation to make this letter a letter of farewell (my motives for writing it lie in quite a different direction) is not very strong. I stood at the window a long time, and pressed my face against the glass, and I more than once felt like frightening the toll collector on the bridge by my fall. But I felt too firm a hold on myself the whole time for the decision to dash myself to pieces on the pavement to be able to depress me to the necessary level. It also seemed to me that by staying alive I should interrupt my writing less—even if one does nothing, nothing, but talk of interruptions—than by dying, and that between the beginning of my novel and its continuation after a fortnight, I might somehow in the factory, in full view of my satisfied parents, move and have my being in the heart of my novel.

My dearest Max, I am putting the whole case before you, not because I want you to judge it, for you are not in a position to have any judgment on it, but since I had firmly decided to jump from my window without writing a letter of farewell—after all one has the right to be tired just before the end—now that I am going to walk back into my room again as its occupant, I wanted to celebrate it by writing you a long letter of meeting again, and here it is.

And now a last kiss and good night, so that tomorrow I can do what they want of me, and be the boss of the factory.

From Max Brod, *Franz Kafka: A Biography*, translated by G. Humphreys Roberts and Richard Winston. New York: Schocken Books, 1960. Pp. 91–93. Reprinted by permission of the publisher. Copyright © 1960 by Schocken Books Inc.

Sokel's Comments

At the time Kafka wrote *The Metamorphosis*, his own life situation resembled to an astonishing degree Gregor

Samsa's just before his metamorphosis. This is revealed
by several of his diary entries from the fall of 1912 and
especially by a letter Kafka wrote to Max Brod on
October 8, 1912, which caused Brod to intervene with
Kafka's mother. Besides his work in the insurance office,
which was hateful enough, Kafka also had to take on
additional duties in the factory belonging to his father
and brother-in-law. Now all his free time for writing
was gone, just at a time when, with "The Judgment,"
he had made a breakthrough into his mature literary style
and needed all his time for writing. This additional
burden had been imposed on him by his family, and his
resentment ran deep. He hated his family in these fall
months of 1912 as perhaps never before or since. His
family drove him to despair; and his depression was
the more severe as he knew perfectly well that it was his
fear of his father and his guilt feelings which delivered
him into this slavery. At the time he was quite close to
committing suicide.

There are, in this letter, a number of factors which
went directly into *The Metamorphosis*, composed a few
weeks later. Just as Kafka felt himself responsible for
his family's factory adventure, Gregor, too, assumed the
responsibility of paying off his parents' "debt" or "guilt"
[*Schuld*], and is now being consumed by impotent resentment against this burden which enslaves him to his
boss. As in Kafka's family, so too in the Samsa family
there is no one except the unmarried son to rescue the
family through toil and the sacrifice of his personal life.
His father's growing "unhappy and ill" is linked with the
embitteredness and the peevish and stubborn senility of
old Mr. Samsa. Suicide seems to Kafka, it is true, a "rejecting" of all responsibility and hence a liberation, but
at the same time a betrayal on all sides—a betrayal of the
family and a betrayal of writing. In the same way, it is
true, the metamorphosis is a rejection of all responsibility,
but it is, at the same time, a betrayal of the family. As
Kafka's suicide would rob him of the chance to test himself in both hostile camps—of literature and of life—so
the metamorphosis cheats Gregor of the rewards which

a conscious retreat into inwardness could bring him. The dominant element in both cases is bitterness and negative feeling toward the family, and guilt feelings toward it as well. In *The Metamorphosis*, too, as in Kafka's letter, it is "the youngest sister" from whom Gregor at first expects help and sympathy, but against whom his rage quite consciously directs itself before turning against the whole family.

From Walter H. Sokel, *Franz Kafka: Tragik und Ironie*. Munich and Vienna: Albert Langen, Georg Müller, 1964. Pp. 86–88. [Trans. S. C.] By permission of the publisher. Copyright © 1964 by Albert Langen Georg Müller Verlag GmbH, Munich and Vienna.

Two conversations between Kafka and Gustav Janouch, 1920–1923

I took the English book out of my jacket pocket and put it in front of Kafka on the bedcover. . . . When I said to him that Garnett's book [*Lady into Fox*] copied the method of the *Metamorphosis*, he smiled wearily and remarked, with a small disclaiming movement of his hand, "Oh no! He doesn't get it from me. It's in the times. We both copied it from that. The animal is closer to us than man. That is the cage. Relationships are easier with animals than with men."

From Gustav Janouch, *Gespräche mit Kafka*. Frankfurt am Main: S. Fischer, 1968. P. 43 [Trans. S.C.] Reprinted by permission of the New Directions Publishing Corporation. Copyright © 1968 by S. Fischer Verlag GmbH, Frankfurt am Main.

•   •   •

My friend Alfred Kampf . . . admired Kafka's story *The Metamorphosis*. He described the author as "a new, more profound and therefore more significant Edgar Allan Poe."

During a walk with Franz Kafka on the Altstädter Ring I told him about this new admirer of his but aroused neither interest nor understanding. On the contrary, Kafka's expression showed that any discussion of his book was distasteful to him. I, however, was filled with a craving for discoveries, and so I was tactless.

"The hero of the story is called Samsa," I said. "It sounds like a cryptogram for Kafka. Five letters in each word. The S in the word Samsa has the same position as the K in the word Kafka. The A . . ."

Kafka interrupted me.

"It is not a cryptogram. Samsa is not merely Kafka, and nothing else. *The Metamorphosis* is not a confession, although it is—in a certain sense—an indiscretion."

"I know nothing about that."

"Is it perhaps delicate and discreet to talk about the bedbugs in one's own family?"

"It isn't usual in good society."

"You see what bad manners I have."

Kafka smiled. He wished to dismiss the subject. But I did not wish to.

"It seems to me that the distinction between good and bad manners hardly applies here," I said. "*The Metamorphosis* is a terrible dream, a terrible conception."

Kafka stood still.

"The dream reveals the reality, which conception lags behind. That is the horror of life—the terror of art. But now I must go home."

He took a curt farewell.

Had I driven him away?

I felt ashamed.

From Gustav Janouch, *Conversations with Kafka*, translated by Goronwy Rees. New York: New Directions Publishing Corporation, 1969. Pp. 55–56. Reprinted by permission of New Directions Publishing Corporation. Copyright © 1969 by New Directions Publishing Corporation.

Kafka to his Father, November 1919 *

[Kafka puts these words into his father's mouth:]
What you are, in fact, set upon is living entirely on me.
I admit that we fight with each other, but there are two
kinds of fighting. There is chivalrous fighting, in which
the forces of independent opponents are measured against
each other, each one remaining alone, losing alone, win-
ning alone. And there is the fighting of vermin, which not
only sting but at the same time suck the blood too to
sustain their own life. That is, after all, what the professional soldier really is, and that is what you are. You are
unfit for life; but in order to be able to settle down in it
comfortably, without worries and without self-reproaches,
you prove that I have deprived you of all your fitness for
life and put it into my pockets. What does it matter to
you now if you are unfit for life, now it is my responsibility, but you calmly lie down and let yourself be hauled
along through life, physically and mentally, by me.

From "Letter to His Father," in *Dearest Father:
Stories and Other Writings*, translated by Ernst Kaiser
and Eithne Wilkins. New York: Schocken Books, 1954.
P. 195. Reprinted by permission of the publisher.
Copyright © 1954 by Schocken Books Inc.

Entries in Kafka's Diaries

October 20, 1913

I am now reading *The Metamorphosis* at home and
find it bad.

From *The Diaries of Franz Kafka, 1910–1913*,
translated by Joseph Kresh. New York: Schocken

---

* This letter was never sent. [S.C.]

January 19, 1914

Great antipathy to "Metamorphosis." Unreadable ending. Imperfect almost to the foundation. It would have turned out much better if I had not been interrupted at the time by the business trip.

CRITICAL ESSAYS

Wilhelm Emrich

Franz Kafka

The Animal as Liberating "Self"

A. MODERN ALIENATION AND ITS "LAW"

It is in the early story "Wedding Preparations in the Country," from the period 1906–1907, that the process of alienation still taking place in the working and metropolitan society of today is, to begin with, reflected upon. The hero, Eduard Raban (cover name for Kafka), is standing on the street of a metropolis with the intention of going to the railroad station. It is raining. A lady on the opposite side of the street "now looked at him. She did it casually, and, besides, perhaps she was merely watching the rain coming down in front of him" (H 8).* In the second version, it is said of this lady, "Without intending to, she seemed strange to all the passers-by, as if because of a law" (H 33).

By "law," the young Kafka hence understood nothing other than the force of collectively anonymous, unknown occurrences, hidden from the will and the "intention" of the individual—occurrences which alienate people from one another. This force is represented here by "one's work," by an existence in the "office," an existence that splits man off into two spheres: an official one and a private one. This point of view emerges unequivocally from Raban's immediately following trains of thought:

---

* H = Franz Kafka, *Hochzeitsvorbereitungen auf dem Lande und andere Prosa aus dem Nachlass* (Frankfurt, 1953), translated by Ernst Kaiser and Eithne Wilkins as *Dearest Father: Stories and Other Writings* (New York, 1954). [S.C.]

"Well, then," he reasoned, "if I could tell it to her, she wouldn't be at all surprised. One overworks at the office to such an extent that one is too tired even to enjoy one's vacation properly. But for all the work one does, one still doesn't gain any right to be treated with loving kindness by everyone; on the contrary, one is alone, a perfect stranger to everyone, and merely an object of curiosity. And as long as you say *one* instead of *I*, it's of no consequence, and the story can be recited, but as soon as you admit to yourself that it is you yourself, then you are actually pierced to the quick and are horror-stricken" (H 8).

*   *   *

As Raban now grows conscious of this cleavage between the impersonal "one" and the "I," and as he inquires into this "self," he feels himself "actually pierced to the quick and [is] horror-stricken." For what else is there upon which his "I" can be grounded, since he must sacrifice everything to the "office," since everything is subject to it?

*   *   *

Raban feels all the events of life as "strange," anonymously collective forces that make him shudder with dread, events that take place meaninglessly and mechanically, that are incomprehensible and alien to him, that he can participate in only with utter loathing; the climax of the hideously grotesque element of the story is reached when this loathing is directed at, of all things, his own "wedding preparations," at his journey to his bride in the country.

B. THE "BEETLE" RABAN

From this extreme tension existing between an impersonal "one" that dominates everything and an unfathomable "I" that sees itself "pierced to the quick," there now develops the following train of thought, one

that leads to the focal point of the peculiar animal transformations in Kafka's works.

"And, what is more, can't I do what I always did in
dangerous undertakings as a child? I don't even need to
go to the country myself; that isn't necessary. I'll send
my fully clothed body. If it goes out the door of the room
falteringly, this faltering is not a sign of fear but a sign of
its nothingness. Furthermore, it is not excitement that
causes my body to stumble on the stairs when it travels
to the country, sobbing, eating its evening meal there in
tears. For I, I shall meanwhile be lying in my bed,
smoothly covered with my yellowish-brown quilt, getting
the breeze that blows through the room from the slightly
open door. The coaches and people on the street ride
and walk hesitantly over the smooth, bare ground, for
I am still dreaming. The coachmen and the people walking are shy and, looking at me, they ask my permission
before each step they are about to take. I encourage
them, and they do not encounter any obstacle. Lying in
bed, I have the form of a large beetle, a stag-beetle or a
cockchafer, I believe. . . . Yes, the large form of a
beetle. I would carry on then as if it were a matter of
my hibernating—and I press my little legs against my
bulging body. And I murmer a small number of words—
those are instructions to my sorrowing body that is standing quite near me, leaning low over me. Before long I am
through—my body bows, flits away, and will accomplish
everything to best advantage while I rest" (H 11–12).

In this way, by abandoning its human existence and
becoming an animal, the "self" gains superiority over
bodies and things. This prehuman animal form of existence (that had already been near and dear to him while
he was still a "child," as a means of rescue in the face of
"dangerous undertakings") gains such superiority, however, only because it occurs while he is in a "dream" state,
in "hibernation." It is then removed from all human reflections and efforts; it "rests," and in such a state of dreamy
sleep it can control and direct bodies, people, even life
in the street outside, and, indeed, in such a way that the

people on the street no longer "encounter any obstacle." It is, therefore, no longer a question of any kind of rational control, but of an unconsciously free and weightless disposition that causes all obstacles to disappear as if of their own accord. What is hereby achieved is freedom from the domination of the impersonal "one" that makes plans, freedom from the domination of the "office," from that of the "dangerous undertakings."

•   •   •

To be sure, this is only a "dreamed of" borderland possibility. . . . True victory lies not in the elimination of consciousness but in the union of free, unconscious existence and conscious existence that arranges and plans.

Hence, in "Wedding Preparations," this dreamy possibility is represented merely as a passing reflection of Raban's, and is in turn abandoned. Raban has to carry his journey through in a thoroughly concrete manner. He cannot leave his self in bed in a dreamy, animal form and send only his empty body to the country. He remains a human being in unresolvable tension.

However, for Kafka this free, animal form of existence has always been a fundamental means of expressing the antinomies of human existence. Animals do not yet live in a state of consciousness that delimits, objectifies, and thereby hypostatizes everything. An animal still finds itself in the "great instinctive feeling of freedom in all directions" (E 188)—no different from the children in "Children on a Country Road." * For Kafka, animal existence is therefore a thoroughly positive sphere that is still present in the interior of man, even if only as a memory of the emotional world and the psychological level of the child. It appears primarily in man's "dreams," in that state in which rational consciousness is excluded. The conflict between animal existence and the rational world

---

* "Children on a Country Road" is the first of the prose poems constituting Kafka's first book, *Meditation.* [S.C.]

of work, therefore, determines many of Kafka's animal stories.

The Beetle in the Story "The Metamorphosis"

In this story the metamorphosis takes place, likewise, in a dream. But everything proceeds in reverse from the way in which it occurs in Raban's metamorphic vision. For Gregor Samsa, the hero of "The Metamorphosis," does not at all desire such a transformation into an animal; on the contrary, it happens to him suddenly—a frighteningly incomprehensible and strange occurrence. He is far from identifying his ego with a beetle, as is the case with Raban. It is true that he too, precisely like Raban, is in a state of unresolved conflict between work and ego. But Samsa does not thoroughly reflect upon this conflict with the same consistency as Raban. Samsa vacillates between the two spheres. On the one hand he is ruled by the rational, plan-making considerations related to his work: he wants to get up and carry his business trip through. "'Just don't stay in bed being useless,' Gregor said to himself" (E 76). * On the other hand, however, he curses his work, "the upset of doing business," the "torture of traveling" (E 72), and he ponders, "How about going back to sleep for a few minutes and forgetting all this nonsense?" (E 71). This "nonsense" refers to his metamorphosis into the beetle—transformation that inwardly he in no way accepts (by contrast with Raban), but actually wants "to forget" in his sleep. Samsa can look upon the dream metamorphosis only as a negative phenomenon that disturbs his daily work routine. The beetle acquires frightful characteristics; it becomes a "monstrous vermin" that is of no

---

* E = Franz Kafka, *Erzählungen* (Frankfurt, 1946), translated by Willa and Edwin Muir as *The Penal Colony: Stories and Short Pieces* (New York, 1948). Throughout this essay all translations from *The Metamorphosis* are my own. Solely for the convenience of cross-reference and by permission of the publisher, they have been substituted for the translations by Sheema Z. Buehne originally appearing in this text. [S.C.]

help to him but merely hampers him. "When Gregor
Samsa woke up one morning from unsettling dreams, he
found himself changed in his bed into a monstrous vermin. . . . 'What's happened to me?' he thought. It was
no dream" (E 71). Samsa, thus, by contrast with Raban
and his vision, is in a waking state. The transformation
that had taken place in his dream—characteristically in
"unsettling" dreams—suddenly overtakes Samsa upon his
waking, as an incomprehensible occurrence that has "happened to him," something that he, accordingly, did not
want, let alone, like Raban, long to have happen. He
shakes it off as "nonsense" and reflects for a long time and
in detail upon his strenuous career, upon his relationship
to the head of his firm; and he considers whether he can
now still catch the seven o'clock train (E 73). It does not
enter his mind at all that he could perhaps be hindered
in his business trip by his transformation. At the outset
this consideration is beyond the scope of his imagination.
For him the metamorphosis is nonexistent. He remains
rooted in the realm of the impersonal "one." The "self"
is a burdensome verminous bug, a monstrous creature of
a nightmare that *cannot* be reality.

Nevertheless, immediately after Samsa awakes, the
meaning of his "unsettling dreams" and thereby, too, the
meaning of the dream metamorphosis becomes obvious
in his very reflections. Samsa complains of his "grueling
job," of the "upset of doing business," "worrying about
changing trains, eating miserable food at all hours, constantly seeing new faces, no relationships that last or get
more intimate. To the devil with it all!" (E 72). He feels
the estrangement, the missing "intimate" associations
with people, exactly like Raban. What is more, he ponders
on the idea that he would like most of all to "have quit
long ago." Only his concern for his parents, who have to
pay back a large debt they owe the head of his firm, has
prevented him until now from having marched up to the
boss and [in Samsa's own words] "spoken my piece from
the bottom of my heart! He would have fallen off the
desk! . . . Well, I haven't given up hope completely;
once I've got the money together to pay off my parents'

debt to him—that will probably take another five or six years—I'm going to do it without fail. Then I'm going to make the big break. But for the time being I'd better get up, since my train leaves at five" (E 73).

There can be no doubt that this conflict, between his occupation and his desire to make the final break and become self-reliant and independent, was the cause of his "unsettling dreams." Since the pressure of the moral obligation of his occupation prevails in this conflict, and since the fulfillment of his desire to become a "self" of his own is put off for five to six years, this desire *must* of necessity be felt as disturbing and as running counter to his work. The possibilities that offer themselves in the "dream" of simply having the "self" remain in bed and freely and independently direct all the goings-on outside in the world, without being pounded to bits in the hustle and bustle of business—the possibility of this as it occurs to Raban is not one that Samsa can accept. Hence he wards it off. But to ward something off is not to overcome it. The self remains where it is. Man can never quite become the impersonal "one." And the meaning of this terrible "metamorphosis" rests in the very fact that this "irremovable" self, the self that is "not to be got rid of," this reality of the ego that struggles against the impersonal "one," suddenly invades Samsa's concrete daily reality, too, in a shocklike manner, and cannot be simply driven away as an apparition and as a dream fabrication. The seemingly fantastic unreality of this "vermin" is that which is actually supreme reality from which no one can escape.

The boldness of this work of Kafka's lies in the resolute consistency with which it lifts the conflict out of the psychologically internal-emotional plane; on this plane it had been dealt with by other poets for centuries—as, for example, in the case of Wilhelm Meister's conflict between a business career and his "mission." * Whereas in

---

* Wilhelm Meister is the hero of Goethe's novels *Wilhelm Meister's Theatrical Mission, Wilhelm Meister's Apprenticeship,* and *Wilhelm Meister, Journeyman: His Years of Travel.* [S.C.]

older literature the conflict takes place in man's inner, contemplative nature in the form of a clash between feelings and the demands of the world, in Kafka man's contemplative inner nature is alienated from itself. It is true that Samsa feels the conflict in himself and reflects on it, just like any normal person, but at the same time Kafka lifts these feelings and reflections out of their frame of reference and radicalizes the conflict as the absolute antinomy between the impersonal "one" and the "self," in the course of which the two realms can no longer be reached and articulated by reflection and feeling; and the reasons for this are to be found in the history of the period.

What is new in Kafka's creative writing and view of the problem is his realization that the "law" of man's alienation remains hidden from modern man, just as in the case of that lady who appears strange "without intending to, as if because of a law." Man has become the slave of the unknown law of the impersonal "one" to such an extent that he does not even know about his own self or his inner life any longer at all; he represses it and cloaks it again and again by means of calculations. Samsa, it is true, feels extremely uncomfortable in his business life; he senses the conflict through and through, but he believes, in turn, that he can get the better of it by means of mere computations of a business nature. He calculates that when he has saved the amount of money he needs for his parents, he can then at last make the "final break" and take the leap, and get away from his business firm. But he has no idea at all of where he will actually leap, of what potential forms of existence he would like to actualize. His own inner being remains alien to him. It is for this reason, therefore, that Kafka gives it a form that is quite alien to him, the form of a verminous creature that threatens his rational existence in an incomprehensible manner. That is the meaning of the peculiar fact that Kafka, again and again, represents man's own inner being—indeed his "actually" innermost being—either in the form of strange objects and animals that frighteningly break into life, or else in the form of absurd court authorities that demand that man give account of his own self, preventing him, likewise, from carrying out his work at the bank—and indeed, ultimately completely ruining his professional career (*The Trial*). One need but compare the first scene of "The Metamorphosis" with the first scene of *The Trial* to perceive the astounding analogy. In *The Trial,* too, the "surprise" attack upon Josef K. by the authorities takes place immediately upon his waking in bed after oversleeping (like Samsa) as a result of failing, in his heavy slumber, to hear the alarm clock. Thereby, in an illuminating manner, these court authorities "gravitate toward" Josef K.'s own "guilt" (P. 15), of which he is ignorant, and must "arrest" him; in the same manner, in the literal sense Gregor Samsa is taken into custody by his monster and "imprisoned"—Gregor speaks of his "imprisonment" (E 101). And Josef K., too, wants to shake off the entire trial by immediately entering the world of his profession.

> I was taken unawares; that's what it was. If I had . . . got up . . . immediately after waking . . . , if I had acted sensibly . . . everything would have been nipped in the bud. But one is so little prepared. At the bank, for example, I am prepared for things; it would be impossible for something of this sort to happen to me there; I have my own attendant who serves me there; the outside telephone and the interoffice telephone are on my desk in front of me; there are always people, associates and officials coming in and out; but apart from that, and above all, at the bank I am always in the continuum of work, and hence I always have my wits about me (P. 31).

The work-world of the impersonal "one" here, too, is meant to cover up the alien self that, in the form of a monstrous, gruesome court of justice, bursts in upon Josef K., just like the horrible insect into which Samsa sees himself suddenly transformed. For this court mirrors the total inner imaginative world not only of Josef K. but of all other human beings. Since the self is not the "inner being" that is understood and that is "one's own," it must assume the form of something that is external and strange; but it must be in the form of something strange that breaks through the laws of the external, empirically-rational everyday world. This is the completely clear and artistically legitimate consequence ensuing from the modern alienating and reifying process. Kafka does not create "surrealist" phenomena but, on the contrary, creates our reality with utter artistic truth.

Furthermore, since Samsa does not accept his dream world, his subconsciously free, instinctively animal-like existence, exempt from the compulsion of calculation, is perverted in him into a "vermin," by contrast with Raban's dream beetle that operates "quietly," that indeed exerts a quieting and liberating influence, originating as it does in childhood's fairy-like imaginings, where animals are wont to assist the child in "dangerous undertakings" and "rescue" him, as is the case in Grimm's fairy tales where animals, "clearing away" all "obstacles," help young princes or simpletons to come through their dangerous ordeals and adventures successfully. Furthermore, in folk fairy tales children or lovers, by instantly transforming themselves into animals or things, can rescue themselves when they are pursued by witches or evil magicians.

In their original form, Kafka's animal figures possess this affirmatively rescuing significance. They represent the subliminal dreamlike world, the state of man *before* he thinks, that part of him that is prehuman and early human, a part that is always present along with everything else within his soul. However, since modern "business" is very much more dangerous, and since man himself puts himself at the mercy of business, he disowns even his own helpers and obstructs his own "deliverance."

The most gruesome aspect of Samsa's fate is not his metamorphosis but the blindness with which everybody treats this metamorphosis. Samsa will not admit it. "I'll get dressed right away, pack up my samples, and go" (E 88). His parents and his sister do not understand it. The self is what is absolutely alien, void, and nonexistent, not only in the world of business but also in the world of the family. To be sure, his mother and sister love him dearly. In a touching manner they try at first to improve his condition, to surmount their feelings at the sight of this vermin, to take care of him, to protect him, to see to the comforts of life for him, to preserve or once again evoke what for them was human and lovable in him. But the terrible truth of this short story is the realization that even the "most beautiful," most tender relations among people are founded on illusions. No one knows or suspects what he himself "is," and what the other person "is." Gregor Samsa's parents, for instance, never had any inkling of his conflict, of the "sacrifice" that he was making for their sake: "His parents did not understand this too well; in the course of the years they had formed the conviction that Gregor was set for life in this firm" (E 89). They had never dreamed that there was trouble brewing within Gregor, that something had been "out of order" long before the eruption of this inner sickness in the form of the metamorphosis. They did not know that the essential in man can actually be concealed, distorted, and destroyed if he is provided with no more than the "necessaries of life." Now that the distortion assumes visible features, they are at a loss and feel their son to be a "foreign body."

By the same token, however, Gregor had also been mistaken in his relations with his family.

"What a quiet life the family has been leading," Gregor said to himself, and while he stared rigidly in front of him into the darkness, he felt very proud that he had been able to provide such a life in so nice an apartment for his parents and his sister. But what now if all the peace, the comfort, the contentment were to come to a horrible end? (E 95).

He believed he had to provide his family with a pleasant, contented, secure life by sacrificing himself, by selling himself to his business. The reciprocal relationships are based upon secret calculations and compromises, the consequences of which are no longer even suspected by anyone. The semblance of an orderly system and of a "contented" world is created. However, in Gregor's troubled dreams this semblance is torn asunder, and out of the ensuing rent truth arises in the shape of the monstrous verminous insect. Through his "sacrifice" Gregor had distorted his own self. The immolated animal now becomes visible in a merciless distortion.

The deception goes still further. In reality Gregor's parents did not need the sacrifice at all. His father possessed more money than Gregor knew about. His father, too, was able to work and was by no means so ill as it had appeared. Even Gregor was deceived. His sacrifice was meaningless. The family's whole happiness and contentment were founded on deception and covert calculation. The business world invaded even one's private life. Everything rested on "possessions" and "assets," not on "being" (cf. H 42–43). The entire idyll of the family was a lie; nowhere was there "truth." The more money Gregor had given his family, the cooler the relationship between them had grown: "They had just gotten used to it, the family as well as Gregor, the money was received with thanks and given with pleasure, but no special feeling of warmth went with it any more" (E 102). Only now, in Gregor's deformation, does the immolated animal become visible, but that is the very reason why it must be driven away. The monster must disappear, "the stuff next door has to be gotten rid of" (E 141), for only through falsehood can the world continue to survive. Gregor himself must demand this. "He thought back on his family with deep emotion and love. His conviction that he would have to disappear was, if possible, even firmer than his sister's" (E 136). When Gregor "croaks," the idyllic lie continues unchecked in an intensified form. "Three jobs" are in store for them, and a marriageable daughter "stretched her young body." The "horrible end" overtook only Gregor, and it came upon him for the very reason that he wanted to provide for his family.

However, his metamorphosis into an animal has a positive meaning, too. When the beetle Gregor hears his sister playing the violin, there is this decisive statement: "Was he an animal, that music could move him so? He felt as if the way to the unknown nourishment he longed for were coming to light" (E 130). Here is where the meaning of this transformation into an animal first becomes clear. The matter at issue is the "unknown nourishment" that does not exist on earth. As an animal he is at the same time more than an animal. His alienation had the purpose of awakening in him the "longing" for this "nourishment." For Kafka, music had always been a way of sweeping man beyond all earthly limits. In as early a work as the "Investigations of a Dog" it is a matter of combining the science of music with that of dietetics, of enticing down from above, with the help of music, that nourishment that does not originate on earth, and of developing a "doctrine of singing that summons down nourishment from above" (B 289). And this doctrine is to end in an "ultimate science that made freedom valued above all else" (B 290). The final intent of Gregor's metamorphosis into a beetle is the escape into freedom, that longing for man's "unknown nourishment."

The animal, or rather the monster of this "metamorphosis," thus designates a sphere that can never be expressed, and, what is more, that cannot even be seen. For not one of the people involved actually sees the animal. In spite of all the realism in the description of this animal, the animal itself can never be understood, and a visual image of it can never be gained. It is beyond all power of human comprehension by empirical means.

•   •   •

It would be meaningless to interpret Samsa the beetle as a real beetle. Kafka himself formulated this unequivocally: When the publishing firm of Kurt Wolff planned to put out "The Metamorphosis" and had Ottomar Starke prepare an illustration for it, Kafka wrote to the publisher on October 25, 1915, saying, "It has . . . occurred to me that he [O. Starke] might want to draw the insect itself. Not that, please, not that! I do not wish to restrict his scope, but I wish only to request it as a result of my better understanding of the story, as is natural. The insect itself cannot be drawn. It cannot be drawn even as if seen from a distance."

Gregor's hypostatized dream is at the same time more

than a dream, for even dream figures could, if need be, still be copied. It is the mystery that everything talks about and that is nevertheless ineffable. In a "parable," however, such a mystery is unveiled. Truth becomes manifest: ". . . you would yourselves have become parable" (B 96). Samsa's "metamorphosis" is the entrance of his self into the parable. Only there does his self become "real," only there does it demolish the falsehood of the human world.

What, then, is the beetle Samsa? It is obviously something that is felt to be unbearable, alien, and frightening by *everyone*, including even Gregor Samsa. For even he, to begin with, does not identify with this beetle. Although he becomes subject to it and has no choice but to assume a beetle's mode of life, he is, at first, caught in the thoughts, ideas, and emotions of his former life, and he feels it painful to be no longer able to make himself understood. To be sure, existing as a beetle thrusts him out of everything that he is used to and makes him alien and frightening to everyone. But his attachment to the world around him is not thereby diminished, not even by the fact that his family's actual financial circumstances, hitherto kept hidden from him, are now made manifest. He would like to return to his old life, but is prevented from doing so by the incomprehensible force of his beetle-existence. Hence, even his sister, who has loved him very much and has taken care of him, finally says with justice, "It has to go; that's the only answer, Father. You just have to try to get rid of the idea that it's Gregor" (E 134).

However, as his longing for music and for the unknown nourishment has already shown, Gregor finally does nevertheless free himself from his enslavement by the empirical world. His death is not merely a meaningless annihilation, but a liberating realization. Gregor says "Yes," to his own death. He dies reconciled with himself and with the world.

He thought back on his family with deep emotion and love. His conviction that he woud have to disappear was, if possible, even firmer than his sister's. He remained

in this state of empty and peaceful reflection until the
tower clock struck three in the morning. He still saw
that outside the window everything was beginning to
grow light (E 136).

Nowhere within the substance of the tale, of course,
is any mention of this realization made; nowhere, likewise, is there any intimation of the nature of the
"unknown nourishment" referred to—whether what is
meant is spiritual, religious, psychological, or even purely
physical. Since we have hitherto—in conjunction with
Raban's formulation that he "himself" remained at home
as a beetle and sent merely his clothed body to the country—spoken of the fact that Samsa's masked "self," a self
that is hidden from him, appears in his troubled dreams
as a beetle, some clarification is needed.

It is no longer possible to understand this "self" psychologically, as a determinable psychic state that can
be explained in terms of the realm of feelings, wishes,
hopes, dreams, strivings, etc.; somewhat in the sense,
perhaps, that in the conflict with his business occupation
there arise against the world of work and the world of
family a series of "inner" emotions, ideals, and goals
which now represent, as it were, Samsa's "actual" self
that until now had been suppressed. That is out of the
question. Besides, in that case, it would be altogether
impossible to understand how such an inner life could
assume—of all forms—the form of a disgusting verminous
insect. Even in the view developed by us—that, unlike the
Raban vision, it is a matter of a perversion of the self,
since this self is suppressed or opposed by Samsa and
must therefore assume negative characteristics—such a
psychological interpretation is not possible. For, in that
event, Samsa inwardly would have to come to terms
with his suppressed self. This self would have to develop
content and meaning that would have appeal for him,
force him to adopt a point of view, and "transform" him
inwardly, in either a positive or a negative sense. But no
statement whatsoever is made with respect to such
psychic changes and transformations. The "metamor-

phosis" does not take place as a transformation of spirit, mind, or character. This is what is unprecedented and incomprehensible in this story, and what distinguishes it from all former literature dealing with man's heart and mind.

Accordingly, the thesis that the beetle-animal represents the dreamlike unconscious, animal and prehuman, sphere of instinct in man must be decidedly limited or modified. To be sure, this animal is born as it were in a dream; for "when Gregor Samsa woke up one morning from unsettling dreams, he found himself changed in his bed into a monstrous vermin." The metamorphosis, thus, had already taken place before his waking, while he was still in the state of sleeping and dreaming. The dream—that is, the state of being freed of the pressure of diurnal consciousness—is, it is true, the prerequisite for the metamorphosis. But nothing passes over from the dream world into the metamorphosed state. Samsa's beetle-existence by no means shows any condition present in dreams; it shows nothing of a free, instinctively certain immediacy of feeling, of reacting, of experiencing—not even in the sense of its perversion in the form of anxiety dreams or in the form of immediate reactions that, perhaps threateningly, cut across rational diurnal conceptions. For in the very midst of his beetle-existence, he is still swayed by his diurnal conceptions.

Such obvious and understandable interpretations all miss fire. The beetle is, and remains, something "alien" that cannot be made to fit into the human ideational world. That alone is its meaning. It is "The Other," "The Incomprehensible," pure and simple, beyond the reach of any feeling or imagining. "It cannot be drawn even as if seen from a distance," not only in the sense of pictorial art, but also in the sense of imitative interpretation. It is interpretable only as that which is uninterpretable.

And only as such does it contain truth. For whatever "stems from a foundation of truth, must conclude again in the inexplicable" (H 100). Truth and the self are identical. The "self" is the inexplicable, pure and simple.

It is beyond all our conceptions of the self. The beetle embodies a world beyond our conscious as well as our unconscious imagination. The animal, although it is nothing but man "himself," is the absolute disaffirmation of the so-called "human" world. The cleavage between the world in which Samsa lives and Samsa's beetlehood is the cleavage between "imagining" and "being." Since for Kafka the world beyond "imagining" is in man himself, since there is no "beyond" exterior to man, the "image," the "parable" of this beyond is necessarily an earthly image that is unearthly and that at the same time cannot be "drawn." The paradox of these circumstances is the reason why Kafka represents such a beyond in the form of things or animals that incomprehensibly break into everyday existence, causing bewilderment and fright, or abolishing all "obstacles." The perverting of Raban's beetle to Samsa's verminous insect is merely the inversion of the angle of vision.

Raban saw the world from the vantage point of the motionlessly tranquil self and of the foundation of truth. To him the world was bound to appear perverted, intolerable, and disgusting; he was seized with horror at the mere thought of exposing himself to it. Samsa, on the contrary, wishes to remain in the world. For him and for his environment, therefore, the tranquil self must appear as a terrible monster that tears him out of his beloved surroundings. *Both* positions are defensible. Only both together constitute human life. Kafka criticizes and affirms both. It would be mistaken to insist upon interpreting Kafka only through Raban's hermitry, or interpreting him only through Samsa's concern about family and career. Both cross one another in Kafka, just as the names of both, Raban and Samsa, are cover names for his own name (J 26, T 297).* Only when both beetle-visions are interpreted can the full meaning be revealed.

----

* J = Gustav Janouch, *Gespräche mit Kafka* (Frankfurt, 1951), translated by Goronwy Rees as *Conversations with Kafka* (New York, 1969). T = Franz Kafka, *Tagebücher 1910–1923* (Frankfurt, 1951).

Ralph Freedman

Kafka's Obscurity

Within this framework of realism and deliberate distortion Kafka's fiction evolves as a *problem-solving activity*. Man is confronted by a world of impossible dimensions and he cannot but despair of comprehending its overwhelming and mysterious forces. All he can do is to test—and to investigate the effects of his tests—his own capacity for understanding. Each fateful confrontation of the antagonists, self and world, brings with it hosts of mutually exclusive, indeed, paradoxical relations, riddles which seem to clarify but which eventually confound even further man's impossible task of penetrating the puzzling relations of his world. These "riddles" are philosophical and theological, psychological and social; they extend to all spheres of human existence involved in man's search.

Kafka recognized that in the ordinary course of life we are blind to these puzzles because we are unaware. Only a specific, peculiarly decisive event, as Wilhelm Emrich suggests, makes us aware of ourselves and challenges our capacity for understanding.* The arrival at the Castle, the arrest in *The Trial*, the summons to the captain in *Amerika*, all of these are events which change the expected order of things and lead to the significant distortion. From this point on, Kafka follows all leads with rigorous logic.

To allude to Kafka's affinity with naturalistic form, this

---

* "Franz Kafka," *Deutsche Literatur im Zwanzigsten Jahrhundert* (Heidelberg: Wolfgang Rothe Verlag, 1956), pp. 328 ff.

method appears as an intensified version of Zola's pre-
scriptions in *Le Roman expérimental*. The objective
author-observer introduces his character into a carefully
specified world. Keeping all elements constant, he then
observes his character's adjustment to a particular change.
Heller's God paneling the walls of the cave with mirrors
is the writer himself, seeking to extract a particular meaning from his deliberately reconstructed encounter between protagonist and world. *

"The Metamorphosis" illustrates this manner most
clearly. The significant shift, of course, is Gregor's
awakening in the shape of a stag-beetle. The story develops all consequent changes in both the hero and the
world. As in *Gulliver's Travels*, once an initial change
is accepted, all else follows with convincing logic.

The hero's transformation and the change in his relations to the world involve significant cognitive changes.
Kafka's way of exploring the paradoxes Gregor confronts
is therefore at first epistemological; that is, it is concerned
with different ways of knowing reality, of exploring the
shifting relations between self and world. From Gregor's
point of view, the tragedy of "The Metamorphosis" consists in the self's gradual reduction to its most vital center
—its self-consciousness. In two stages—a more superficial
change in spatial relations and a more central change in
the consciousness of time—Gregor is finally reduced to
a mere speck of self-awareness which is ultimately extinguished. As in Swift's book, the story begins with shifts
in cognitive relations and ends in a crucial change in
the nature of the hero himself.

Immediately following the awakening, only physical
appearances and perspectives seem to be changed while
Gregor's essential self appears unchanged. With meticulous care and a great deal of fantastic realism, Kafka
portrays shifts in spatial relations which suddenly cir-
cumscribe Gregor's movements and world. His bed is an
immense obstacle. He can hardly reach the door-handle.

---

* Erich Heller, *The Disinherited Mind* (New York: Farrar,
Straus, 1957), pp. 199–200. [S.C.]

His voice gradually transforms itself from a human voice to an animal squeak, while his memory and other mental faculties as a human being seem to remain essentially unimpaired. But more and more the trappings of humanity disappear, helped by the ill-concealed outrages of his employer and his family. Transformations now affect Gregor more substantially; his vision adjusts to his new perspectives. The room seems too big; the furniture oppresses him. He prefers closed windows and dirt. His sister perceives him sitting in an animal-like trance. But these changes are not wholly generated from within Gregor's transformed shell. They are also conditioned by the world's reactions to his condition.

The mortal wound inflicted by the father with the unfortunate apple provides a second shift in relations which affects the core of Gregor's self. The wound eats more and more deeply towards the center of his self, his human consciousness and memory. Before this event, appearances in self-perception and in perceptions of him by others undergo important shifts, but time continues to strike the hours with the alarm-clock's exactness. Gregor's sense of time is almost unchanged. But after his last foray into humanity, his fatal wound, his last response to his sister's music, self-consciousness begins to dim and, with it, his sense of time. In the end, the obliteration of time coincides with Gregor's obliteration.

Gregor's reduction to a "mere" self, and his consequent destruction, are conditioned by parallel changes in the external world. These changes occur in response to Gregor's mysterious *Verwandlung*. The father's assumption of "authority" by becoming a uniformed bank-messenger is the most obvious illustration, but equally important are changes which lead to the constriction of the household. The cleaning woman fully transforms Gregor's room into a garbage dump and becomes another mortal enemy. The entire home assumes an atmosphere of degradation as even the mother and sister "adjust" to the new condition. The three "lodgers"—whatever else they may be thought to signify—typify this oppressive shift in Gregor's former world. An unindividuated

"chorus," introduced in a manner reminiscent of romantic
and expressionistic fiction, they suggest the intrusion of
an entire alien world. They push the family into the
kitchen, usurp the dining-room and are treated by
Gregor's parents with exaggerated deference. The world
has been wrenched out of recognition. For the helplessly
observing Gregor, its change has become irrevocable.

Shifts in both self and world condition and require
one another. Gregor's own transformation had also been
a function of his world. He had in fact been a vermin,
crushed and circumscribed by authority and routine,
before the actual transformation had taken place: Gregor
recalls that when the manager had towered above him
in the office he had already felt like an insect. Moreover,
we noted that the most important changes had been
evoked by others' reaction to his condition: his rejection
by boss, father, even by his mother and sister. But it is
crucial to this revelation of his condition—appearing more
and more purely as he nears his end—that it had been an
aspired condition. He had been imprisoned in his animal
existence which had been implied by his human life, yet
freed from intolerable burdens, including the tyranny of
time. In his death likewise he is both extinguished and
set free.

If Gregor's end is marked by a constriction of his physical universe and a paradoxical liberation from the bond-
age of himself (the true and final transformation of the
hero), the family, we infer, had been similarly constricted
and set free. In this way, relations constantly shift, unite,
and contrast with one another. The self and the various
figures representing the world are equally important,
and the author focuses on them simultaneously. For this
reason, the shift in point of view to the family is a perfectly defensible way of concluding the story. Gregor's
extinction has, in the end, become the family's liberation.
Since the self has been obliterated by the world, the
emphasis must now be placed upon the world, for its
figures have gained at last the liberation the hero had
sought. Grete's yawn of freedom neatly ties the story to
the transformation of the beginning. Yet this very con-

clusion has pushed us to the point of absurdity—reached by the simultaneous creation and dislocation of a particular world—in which contradictory solutions, like constriction and freedom, obliteration and awareness of existence, equally apply.

From Ralph Freedman, "Kafka's Obscurity: The Illusion of Logic in Narrative." *Modern Fiction Studies*, VIII: 1 (Spring 1962). Pp. 65–67. Copyright © 1962 by Purdue Research Foundation, Lafayette, Indiana. Reprinted by permission of Purdue Research Foundation.

Edwin Honig

The Making of Allegory

Or take the example of Kafka's *Metamorphosis*. The structure of oppositional relationships is not more complex than in *The Faerie Queene*. It is conditioned differently; that is, by a realistic milieu instead of a mythicized fairyland. Yet Kafka's localization is significantly deceptive, for it is really an emanation of the hero's own disabled consciousness. Only through this inward focus are the scene and characters realized, although the objective tone of the narrative, emphasizing the exigent event and the action of others, makes the focus and relationship appear to be outward.

Like Spenser's Knights of Holiness and Temperance, who are designated in their missions at the start, Kafka's Gregor Samsa has already been judged when the story begins. That judgment and the self-punishment it entails are the conditions the story undertakes to dramatize. In Spenser the relationship of man to society is partly established in the feudal obligations of the knights to their queen, and partly in the Christian nature of their missions, where the particular virtue they enact is manifested. In *The Metamorphosis* this relationship, always at stake and continually being questioned, is reduced to one concerning a man and his immediate family. Authority rests with the father and the social injunction to work, which he represents. (In *The Castle* Kafka asks, "Does not the least degree of authority contain the whole?") Gregor's "crime"—his sudden and inexplicable inertia—immediately causes his metamorphosis. From a state of social and filial obligation, centered in his work as the family's indefatigable breadwinner, he falls into an

138

animal-like lethargy—i.e., he lies down on the job. From the beginning, then, it is both his punishment and the means of his *éclaircissement* to contend with himself and others as a giant insect equipped with human consciousness.

The darkness out of which Gregor emerges transformed is on one level the darkness of a former life, a guilty sleep—the sleep of an impossibly routinized and self-alienated existence. The life to which he awakes when the story opens is the frightening life of new awareness. He has dreamed himself, perhaps unconsciously wished himself, completely out of social usefulness. Of course, as it soon becomes clear, he has wished himself out of the sort of social usefulness imposed upon him without his conscious assent—without his having been permitted to choose the kind of work which would be both possible and right for him. His dilemma is that he must challenge, grapple with, and seek protection from the judgment that society places on him for deserting his work, and at the same time accept the judgment, the guilt he actually feels, "lying down." On this level, the physical equivalent of the social and psychological metamorphosis—and the overt sign of his rebellion and ostracism—is what he becomes to his family and to himself as he lies in bed: simply a huge, detestable insect.

Precisely because his metamorphosis is so unmistakable, Gregor can now summon his past life into consciousness. Abandoned to animal abjectness and mere spectatorship, he begins to understand the "human" condition as he represents it. And since his separation from the family has been made manifest, he can now try to come to terms with his alienated condition and his inarticulate yearnings. We are gradually made to see him, almost literally in the mosaic vision of an insect, reflecting the totality of many fragmentary bits of behavior toward him on the part of his office superior, his sister, his mother, his father, the family boarders, and finally the charlady. As he is seen by each in turn, there is a cumulative and recapitulative sense which confirms his physical metamorphosis. The effect is simultaneously

to strip down to its essential absurdity the inadequacy
of their responses as well as to exhibit him becoming
exactly what each takes him for.

To his sister, who seems closest to him, he is most
unequivocally understood in his animal needs. She brings
him the garbage he relishes and battens on. To his office
superior, the chief clerk, he is that unheard-of monster
who broke the rule of punctuality—even so, the most negli-
gible of all the impossibly stringent rules of office routine. The father, whose complete lack of self-discipline
makes him lean on others, exaggerates the authority he
does not use on himself, so that when imposed on others
it becomes a terrible virtue covering and compensating
for his own defects. Thus when Gregor's father beats
him back with a stick and hysterically pelts him with
apples, Gregor encounters the punishment by which a
purblind authority asserts itself and grows strong. And,
as a result of Gregor's metamorphosis, his father, formerly
a sick, useless old man, turns into a vigorous job-holding
bank official. When Gregor's metamorphosis is accepted
as a fact, the other characters show themselves for what
they are. The mother is without real understanding in
her compassion. The intrusive boarders insultingly evalu-
ate the situation, and this in turn calls forth the wrath of
the father, who in driving them out of the house unifies
the family against Gregor. It is as though the family
needed first to have the goad of the boarders' social
disapprobation in order to swallow its own distaste and
personal chagrin, before finally expressing its own real
feelings overtly. At the end, the charlady, moved by
malice, prods Gregor's dying body with a broom; having
no organized system of "values" to propel her upward,
she can only demonstrate her frustrations in such forms
of gratuitous revenge.

The metamorphosis which started within the hero's
consciousness earlier now becomes the gross outward
fact of his physical transformation. This exposure of an
exaggerated debasement gradually provokes a series of
reactions among successive characters, who thereby assist
in dramatizing the hero's identity. The identification pro-

ceeds step by step, and at each development we see how
the central metaphor (metamorphosis) relates to, and
finally overwhelms, the hero's awareness.

Answering Gregor's need for love and understanding
there is shame, expressed by his sister's covert recognition
of his animal needs, while his mother can only grieve
mutely for the old Gregor, whom she pictures in the
illusory past he has discarded. Repudiating Gregor's
anxious industry and personal merit as a jobholder is the
machinery of institutionalized legalities represented by
the chief clerk. In response to Gregor's need for guidance
and support is the rivalry of the father and the authori-
tarian justice he wrathfully voices. Gregor's situation is a
limbo where the forces of oppositional entities—dark-
light, animal-human, lust-love, seeming-being, despair-
faith—are constantly refracted through his consciousness
and exposed in his immediate surroundings. Since he
cannot assert any actual sense of himself, he falls prey
to those forces in himself and in others that have hope-
lessly mistaken him. It is as if he negatively and in-
evitably "self-awares" himself out of existence on learning
how arbitrary his identity is; or how, in depending so
largely on others, it must perish for lack of the right
sustenance. If the social dispensation, typified by the self-
preservation of the family, is pre-eminent, who then is
the individual alone? The story seems to answer the
question by ironically posing another: Nobody?

And yet, as seen through the dramatization of his needs
and failures, Gregor's identity and the problematic issue
it raises are developed in the distorted relationship between himself and others, which he has permitted or
encouraged to grow. This may be put in the form of
another question: What has he actually given of himself that he should expect others, with similar needs, to
give something in return? In such terms, the final criticism
seems not to be leveled against society so much as
against Gregor, who sinks into his dilemma because he
is unable to find his real self. The fact that each character
in the story may be taken as a personification of some
particular defect, essentially related to Gregor's instiga-

tive needs, becomes the core of the criticism. All the characters thereby show their own deadly stultification, including Gregor in his bug-like form—the last degree of the process.

What Gregor reveals of himself through others, in their particular attributes, accounts for the outward direction of the allegory from an inward focus. This reverses the process in traditional allegory, which starts with the personified attribute, and by lending it urgency and vitality works inward to the meaning of the attribute in a pre-established moral context. In Kafka everything seems to proceed from the hero's self-judgment at the beginning. He has no vital mission; he has cut himself off from society. Thus, instead of extending his identity, like Una or Red Cross, by active juxtaposition and opposition to others, he constantly dwindles. He is seen, as it were, from the opposite end of the telescope: instead of finding his many actual identities, he shrinks and is finally converted into nothingness.

There is no moral closure in *The Metamorphosis*. It ends with the stark critical question of the individual and society which Gregor's metamorphosis poses. Earnest moralists will of course add what is lacking in the context—that a complete recognition of stultification, the full awareness of guilt or sin or dread, is the abyss of despair, and that its convincing portrayal is enough to make clear the need of a "leap," as the Existentialists call it, to commitment.

Edwin Honig, *Dark Conceit*. New York: Oxford, 1966. Pp. 64–68. © 1959 by Edwin Honig. Reprinted by permission of Oxford University Press, Inc.

Max Bense

Kafka's Conception (*Thematik*) of Being

We have drawn a distinction between the classical conception of being of the theodicy and the non-classical conception of being of existential analysis or fundamental ontology. In the theodicy there is God as first cause, the ground to which all beings are related. In existential analysis man is the subject, the foundation, in relation to whom everything becomes intelligible and interpretable. In the theodicy before Creation God thinks out many possible worlds, but realizes only one of them, and the result of this is that in the classical conception of being there exist at once the ontological problem of the modal distinction of the real world and the epistemological problem of objective reality (*Realitätsgegebenheit*). The existential analysis belonging to fundamental ontology betrays its origin in Husserl's phenomenology, insofar as it retains, throughout, the most important finding of his transcendental egology, namely, the fact that the real world represents an admittedly sufficient but not a necessary condition for the constitution of consciousness.* The existential mode of analysis thus remains basically indifferent to the classical distinction between possible and realized, real and unreal worlds, and accordingly does not know the explicit problem of objective reality.

Summarized, this state of affairs can be expressed

---

* Edmund Husserl (1859–1938), German philosopher and mathematician, as author of the *Logical Investigations* (1900) the chief initiator of the phenomenological movement in philosophy. Philosophy, he maintained, must attend to and grasp things as they are presented, must turn "to things themselves." [S.C.]

more or less in the following way: in the classical conception of being the fiction of a distinctive (*ausge-
zeichnet*) world which represents itself as a real world
is constantly maintained and at best aesthetically and
ethically varied between being and seeming, perfection
and imperfection; in the non-classical conception of being,
on the other hand, this fiction of the distinctive world
is either given up from the start or successively destroyed.
To the extent that for every science indebted to the classical conception of being there exists the problem of the
investigation of the real world or of this or that world
otherwise modally distinctive, each ontological tendency
thus being already modally structured, there is for every
literature indebted to this classical conception of being
the problem of epic realism, which, for example (as
Lukács, who has been working on both the aesthetics
and sociology of literary realism, recently stressed), "old
Fontane" formulated in the following way: "The best
novel would be the one whose characters take their place
among the characters of real life!" [*]

For a science based on the non-classical conception of
being—and it can be shown that large sectors of modern
physics, quantum mechanics, for example, fall under this
aspect—a problem of reality, a problem of the real world
(for example, of the real atom) just as little exists, as
epic realism is a matter for discussion for a literature
based on a non-classical conception of being. What is
called surrealism [. . .] comes under the non-classical
conception of being, in which the fiction of the distinctive, real world no longer exists. And it is certain that
essential parts of Kafka's writings also belong to Sur-

---

[*] Cf. Lukács, "Der alte Fontane," *Sinn und Form*, III: 2 (1951).
[Georgy Lukács, b. 1885, an eminent intellectual historian and
literary critic; most of his life's work has centered on the historical
and theoretical justification and the practical illustration of a subtle
socialist realist aesthetics. The novelist Theodor Fontane (1819–
1898) was the representative in Germany of the great European
bourgeois realist tradition of the 19th century. His novels, which
are the first in German to depict the life of modern urban society,
are distinguished by a lucid, critical impressionism and at once
a skepticism without illusion and traces of socialist belief. S.C.]

realism and constitute surreality in the sense of a world in which the distinction between real and unreal constituents no longer has any ontological meaning. Kafka's diary entry for 1914, according to which "the sense for the representation of my dreamlike inner life . . . has pushed everything else into the background," could stem from the dream-theories of the surrealistic manifestos of Breton.* And so the ontological meaning of Surrealism and accordingly the task of defining it ontologically lies in its implicitly formulated program of a non-classical, literary conception of being, in which the fiction of a distinctive, real world no longer exists and which, accordingly, considers itself exempt from the problem of objective reality in literature, since it no longer sets itself the task of being realistic. To this extent surrealistic literature, based on a non-classical conception of being, is consistent in being neither psychological nor sociological nor mythological in an explicit sense, although it does not reject the devices which prompt such explications. From this it does not follow that surrealism departs on principle from the domain of rationality. The rational structure is in fact as much at home in possible as in real worlds. And in fact even Breton's "Manifesto" speaks of an "absolute rationalism, which has validity now as before." The non-classical surreal conception of being has a thoroughly rational structure of its own. And accordingly the observable, real accuracy of the unreal found in Kafka or his precision with the imaginary [. . .] does not signify an odd state of affairs: rational precision in the unreal is not itself anything unreal, as is confirmed by the impression awoken for example by "the metamorphosis" of Gregor Samsa into a "monstrous vermin." Furthermore, beyond this, "The Hunter Gracchus" who lingers as a dead man

* *Diaries, II*, p. 77. [André Breton, b. 1896, French poet, novelist, and literary editor, member of the Dadaist movement, author in 1924 of the First and in 1930 of the Second Surrealist Manifestos, later became a Communist. Poetry, for the young Breton, is the domain of the marvelous, the occult, which is as real as the extent to which one confides in it. S.C.]

among the living, and *The Castle*, too, with the complete indeterminacy of the mode of being (*Seinslage*) of the castle, are themselves examples of the logical equivalence of all modes in this kind of literature.

In conclusion I might add to this point that thus, on the whole, this surreal, non-classical conception of being by no means deals merely with the "deformation of the natural form of phenomena," as Paul Klee formulated it in 1924 [. . .] in order to explain effects in his own painting—which, however, extend very much beyond this explanation.* The world of aesthetic being, too, distinguishes itself through the play of modes; every neglect of reality favors the multiplicity of possibilities, and every deformation of the form or of the object, which the aesthetic sign lets emerge from the husk of trivial purposes, making it recognizable and communicable, already almost implies a change of mode. Kafka does not deform.

From Max Bense, *Die Theorie Kafkas*. Cologne and Berlin: Kiepenheuer und Witsch, 1952. Pp. 51–54. Reprinted by permission of the publisher. Copyright © 1952 by Verlag Kiepenheuer, Witsch & Co. GmbH. [Trans. S.C.]

---

* Paul Klee, *Über die moderne Kunst*, 1949.

Hellmuth Kaiser

Kafka's Fantasy of Punishment

The works of Franz Kafka, like dreams in their mixture of fantasy and realism, like works of art of the highest order by virtue of the vitality of their language and the cogent clarity of their descriptions, allow the analytic point of view to gain richer insights into the subconscious currents engendering great art than are permitted by perhaps any other literary work.

Comparable to fairy tales and myths for the self-contained character of their symbolic content, they have for the psychologist the advantage over these forms, of embodying the internal vicissitudes of a single personality and therefore of revealing the connections within an entire personality development. [. . .]

In keeping with the nature of an analytic investigation, those psychological facts which come to light will have no bearing on the character of Kafka which expresses itself in conscious actions, thoughts, and words; instead, elements partly or entirely absent from the writer's consciousness will play a major role.

The reader unfamiliar with such investigations must therefore be warned against supposing that by means of them the "real Kafka" will come to light, or that the gestalt of the artist lying closer to consciousness and perceived from a nonanalytic perspective is only a deceptive mask. . . . To do our utmost to rule out misunderstandings, we want to acknowledge explicitly the fact that our assertions refer to an object not figuring in the usual kind of biographical investigation, and we shall assign to the personality, the levels of whose subconscious we seek to examine, the cover-name K., which Kafka usually gives the heroes of his novels. . . .

The Metamorphosis opens as one morning the hero, a young traveling salesman, just about to go on a business trip required by his job, discovers on awakening that he has been transformed into an ugly, disgusting insect (something like a bedbug, but one of course larger than life-size).

No reason is given for this metamorphosis from which its symbolic significance could be derived. We shall therefore study its effects . . . in order to draw some conclusion as to its meaning.

The metamorphosis is preceded by a span of five years, during which time a steady development always proceeding in the same direction takes place in the hero, Gregor Samsa, and in the parental household in which he lives. This development is introduced by the collapse of the father's business . . . , an event which causes Gregor to devote himself to his job with redoubled zeal, so that he soon . . . becomes the breadwinner for his parents and sister. The mother had always been incapacitated by a physical ailment, and the father, obviously emotionally hard hit by his economic failure, sinks into a condition of physical and mental lethargy, in which he neglects his appearance, sleeps a great deal, dozes listlessly, and for the most part just remains still. With the help of a servant girl the sister takes care of the household and for the rest devotes herself to playing the violin. The son, Gregor, whose ambition grows with his success, finally goes so far in his care of his family that he resolves to send his sister to the conservatory, even though this would restrict him professionally. He intends to announce this plan to his sister on Christmas Eve—which at the beginning of the story is just approaching— "without bothering about any objections."

Now the metamorphosis takes place. Gregor is unable to work and finally dies a few months later of voluntary starvation, after realizing that in this condition he is a horror and a worry and burden to his family.

This event has the following effect on the family: the

sister takes a job in an office,* the mother sews underwear for a clothing firm, the father becomes a bank messenger. The story ends with the father, mother, and
daughter making an excursion together, in the course of
which the family's financial situation is discussed and revealed to be relatively good. The closing sentences are
about the parents' budding wishes, which bid fair to
become true, that their "good-looking, shapely" daughter
will be well provided for through marriage with a "good
husband."

But what is most striking is the change which occurs
to the father throughout the course of the story. Almost
an entire page is devoted to its description. From being
an old man the father becomes a bank official "holding
himself very erect," dressed in a "tight-fitting blue
uniform."

Summarized, then, this is the course of events: the son
becomes strong as a result of the business failure of his
father, through his competence cripples his father's
self-esteem and acquisitive sense, and finally takes over
the father's position in the family while the latter sinks
into the degraded state of a dependent, helpless, needy
creature. Following the catastrophic metamorphosis . . .
the same development takes place in reverse; the father
again takes up his position as head of the family, and the
son sinks into the state of useless ballast. . . .

Thus the story depicts the struggle between son and
father as it rises out of the oedipal conflict. And two
phases of this struggle are placed hard by one another:
the first, in which the son has the advantage, and the
second, in which the father defeats the son. Between both
phases stands the metamorphosis as the line of demarca-
tion or, better, as the event which reverses the direction
of development.

Of course the metamorphosis of the son—viewed psychologically—does not signify an external event but an
internal change in the direction of drive. It is a kind
of self-punishment for his earlier competitive striving

---

* Actually a store. [S.C.]

aimed against the father, a withdrawal from the exacting genital position.

The word "punishment" does not seem appropriate, since after all the son has done nothing more than that which a keen sense of family responsibility would have prescribed to anyone in his position.

But we have to take into account the fact that hostile feelings toward the father, precisely because they warrant punishment, were not allowed to be expressed openly in the story. But if we look very closely, we shall still be able to discover their concealed traces. Namely, even when the actions of the son before as well as after the metamorphosis are depicted so as to be beyond reproach,* the behavior of the father is still inspired by a distinct thirst for revenge: this emotion comes to light in the moment when the father has the opportunity and nominal cause to deal aggressively with his son and is not only "furious" but "glad." The masking tendency has had the effect here of clothing the depiction of the son's feelings of hate for the father in the depiction of the father's corresponding emotions toward the son. Considering the nature of our psychological interpretation, this reading is not only a bare possibility but an absolute necessity. For every striking manifestation in poetry must

---

* Strictly speaking, there is an exception even to this. Gregor intends to send his sister to the conservatory without bothering about "any objections." That is, so to speak, his final and boldest wish before the metamorphosis. Over against this, at the end of the story, is the parents' wish to marry off their daughter. And so if Gregor wanted to send his sister to the conservatory, it was not only out of brotherly concern for her musical development, but—as we may conclude precisely from the parents' opposed wish—by tying her to an artistic career to prevent her from marrying. Again, the brother's jealousy of the sister expressed here may have arisen in turn by a displacement of the oedipal jealousy intended for the mother. This idea might find some support in the fact that according to the story Gregor's decision to send his sister to the conservatory is his last thought before the metamorphosis, so that we may gather that it triggers off the metamorphosis. It follows from this that something must be expressed in this decision which is calculated to release strong feelings of guilt and thus the strong need for punishment.

have its psychological basis in the poet's psyche [*Seele*]; nothing essential can be considered to be the contingent characteristic of a "nature" or "environment" which just happens to be so constituted and is then said to be faithfully depicted.

The punishment which K. dictates to himself through his metamorphosis has a dreadful, sinister character. We shall have to isolate its various features.

The animal into which Gregor is transformed is an insect, a loathsome disgusting creature. From the dishes set down in front of him he picks out for himself the ones that are spoiled, rotten, and unfit for human consumption. The rest he doesn't care for. We see here . . . that the animal state denotes a lower, more infantile level of development of the instinctual life. It is no accident that the animal in this case is an insect, i.e. a creature standing . . . [at an extremely low level] on the evolutionary scale. As far as the development of disgust is concerned, there exists at first an anal pleasure, which is entirely free of disgust. With the repression of anal pleasure, a disgust for the feces arises. As long as the repression is not yet consolidated, the disgust is violent, and the object-domain toward which it is directed is indistinct, since every similarity between a pleasurable object and feces is recognized and seized upon as such, and the pleasurable object in question is drawn into the domain of the disgusting. As the repression of anal pleasure is increasingly consolidated, the line dividing what is disgusting from what is not disgusting becomes narrower and more sharply defined, because anal pleasure no longer goes *in search of* the affinity with or similarity to feces. The result of these facts . . . is that the insect of *The Metamorphosis* feels a decided pleasure in things that are unclean and disgusting, hence, in feces, and can therefore enjoy the spoiled food without disgust.

In the light of these considerations, we can speak of the metamorphosis as a regression into the anal phase.

It is worth noting that the triumph of the son over the father is accompanied by the father's growing dirty in precisely the same way that the triumph of the father is accompanied by the son's growing unclean. The son cannot put himself in the father's position without the father's putting himself in the son's position. Uncleanness, anality, is here conceived as a demon which, driven out of one person, must enter into another. The drives which are no longer allowed to take effect in one's actions are projected onto the partner, the "opponent."

Another dimension of the "punishment by metamorphosis" results from the father's behavior toward the son. As we have already stated, the balance of power between father and son is reversed by means of the son's metamorphosis. The father's hitherto suppressed hostility and craving for revenge—the mirror image of the oedipal hate which, as we have concluded, the son bears toward the father—manifest themselves in two aggressive acts, in which the father bodily maltreats the son.

Gregor is first maltreated when after his metamorphosis he attempts in his monstrous form to calm the office manager of his firm, who is enraged by Gregor's absence; and to this end he emerges from his room. The father, infected by the horror which grips the mother as well as the office manager, attempts to scare the "insect" back with angry hissing. Gregor, who in his new condition has only an imperfect control over his body, gets stuck in the door to his room, of which only one wing is open; one of his sides gets scraped raw, and ugly patches remain on the white door:

> . . . when from behind his father gave him a hard shove, which was truly his salvation, and bleeding profusely, he flew far into his room.

The second scene in which he is maltreated is more detailed: the sister intends to clear the furniture out of Gregor's room in order to make it easier for him to crawl around. She also wins her mother over to this plan, although at first the mother, with her instinct for the right thing, has misgivings about it, because such an act would necessarily make the son believe that the family was now convinced of the irreversibility of his present condition. Gregor, who earlier had wanted the furniture removed, finds the clearing out of the things which have become dear to him, now that it is about to become reality, a painful experience, and in the attempt to save at least something, he breaks out of his seclusion. [The action of pp. 35–37 is summarized.] . . . In the living room Gregor is surprised by his father. The father, taking a mistaken view of Gregor's responsibility for the mother's fainting, chases the son around the table and finally bombards him with apples. . . .

There are *two* scenes of maltreatment. In the first scene two injuries occur; in the second, two apples strike. The repeated occurrence of the number two strengthens the interpretation, in any case obvious, that the mistreatments are "acts of castration" [in the broadest psychoanalytical meaning of the term].

In the second scene, too, we find easily interpreted allusions to the sexual basis of the entire proceedings. The behavior of the mother and sister portrays with uncanny accuracy the typical behavior of a well-meaning family toward a member who is neurotically ill. "The furniture is cleared out," i.e. family life becomes oriented to the neurosis. The sick member is granted a special existence, concessions are made to him, partly for his own good, partly to get along with him better, and areas of conflict are removed. The danger inherent in this is hinted at in the story: the individual who has taken flight in regression is robbed by this behavior of his last connections with reality. K. feels this instinctively and, in order to salvage at least something from his former life, takes up a protective position in front of his relation to woman, to sexuality—indeed his position protects it by covering it up. One can adduce from other works of Kafka that fur is for him almost always the symbol of the female genitalia (as this symbol is repeatedly found in folklore), and that for K., only erotically active, aggressive women come into question as love objects. These comments will be sufficient to clarify the meaning of the "picture," which . . . Gregor had cut out of a glossy magazine.

The fact that we are really dealing here with an oedipal conflict, i.e. with jealousy toward the father on account of the mother, is evident from the end of the second occasion of Gregor's maltreatment. . . .

With his last glance he saw the door of his room burst open as his mother rushed out ahead of his screaming sister, in her chemise, for his sister had partly undressed her while she was unconscious in order to let her breathe more freely; saw his mother run up to his father and on the way her unfastened petticoats slide to the floor one by one; and saw as, stumbling over the skirts, she forced herself onto his father, and embracing him, in complete union with him—but now Gregor's sight went dim—her hands at the back of his father's neck, begged for Gregor's life. (39)

Here we find in immediate connection with the father's violent "castrating" intimidation an allusion to the son's witnessing the primal scene, revealed by the typical "paralysis of sight" which corresponds to the effect of repression.

It may seem strange that in the story the metamorphosis, i.e. the regression, takes place first, and only in the further course of this process do the castration shock and the witnessing of the primal scene appear. But if we consider these experiences more precisely . . . we shall find, at least so far as the castration shock is concerned, that they are in no way the original childhood experiences which take place years before regression, but further developments of these impressions, complex structures, which have arisen through the interactions of various strivings within the subconscious. But even where a further development is not recognizable—as in the witnessing of the primal scene—this does not mean that the corresponding primary experience has to be intended, but only a re-emergence of this experience in memory or fantasy. For the symbol-language of literature does not distinguish real experience from the resurgence of the repressed into consciousness.

Until now we have observed two moments of the

punishment by metamorphosis: anal regression and the reactivation of the oedipal situation (castration, witnessing of the primal scene). We now come to a third moment, the most important one for the particular goals of our study.

If during the time of his punishment Gregor is maltreated by his father, suffering the repetition of the castration experience, there is something more in this than the gratification of the need for punishment. The fruit which the father employs while maltreating him—the apple—is indeed the typical, proverbial reward of the child, as it recurs, for example, in "moralizing tales," not to speak of its significance in the biblical fall of man. What the father grants the son with the bombardment is not only punishment, but pleasure, too, and masochistic pleasure at that. We suspect now that what is "startling and unbelievable" about the pain Gregor feels after the apples are thrown is in fact the circumstance that this pain contains pleasure. It is also this pleasure that causes Gregor to feel "as if nailed to the spot" and to "stretch" out his body or, as we can now say, to "stretch himself voluptuously" in a "complete confusion" of all his senses. The confusion originates, of course, in the fact that pleasure and pain are mingled in the most intimate fashion.

In every case the injuries are inflicted on the son from behind. In the first scene it is a "hard shove from behind" which makes him bleed; the apples in the second scene hit him in the back, and one of them even remains lodged there. This points to the fact that the masochism is connected here to the anal sphere, an association which fits in well with the fact that the metamorphosis into a filthy insect represents a regression to anal fixations. One could well imagine that the effects of a chastisement suffered at the hands of the father (blows on the buttocks) have here become associated, on the one hand, with the castration threatened by the father and, on the other hand, with the pleasurable feelings associated with defecation. Out of the encounter of this complex with the excitations arising from the observation of the primal scene, it is possible that as a result the desire has formed for a forcible *impregnation* by the father in the form of a *coitus per anum,* a process described by the scene of the bombardment with apples, if we conceive of it as a rebus or pun. With the aid of parallels from other works of Kafka . . . we can go one step further and assume that the lodging of the apple in the back of the "insect" also signifies a wish fulfillment—namely, by this coitus to gain the father's penis as a substitute for his own lost member.

From Hellmuth Kaiser, "Franz Kafka's Inferno: Eine psychologische Deutung seiner Strafphantasie." *Imago* (1931). Pp. 53–61. [Trans. S.C. and Barney Milstein.] Reprinted by permission of Mr. Mark Paterson, S. Freud Copyright.

Peter Dow Webster

Franz Kafka's "Metamorphosis" as Death and Resurrection Fantasy

Kafka's "Metamorphosis" has fascinated many readers who respond to it on an unconscious level of apprehension rather than on a level of conscious understanding. The tale is as weird as many a nightmare they have had, and as strangely, even humorously disturbing. Here are the eternal ones of the dream or the archetypal constructs of the unconscious subjected to the secondary elaboration and conscious control of the artistic mind. Although most readers feel the import of these characters vaguely, many prefer not to know their total meaning too clearly because of the anxiety involved in facing even artistically created reality; and the revelations of art, like those from the unconscious itself, do challenge and sometimes destroy the frontier defenses of the ego.

Kafka himself took care not to examine too closely his dreams. . . . Because of his refusal or maybe his ego's fear of a total invasion of the unconscious, he continued to pay throughout his life for a deep-seated destructive urge against the mother image and an equally strong desire to possess or to be possessed by this archetypal image. What Kafka presumed, or at least claimed, to be detestation, originating in fear, of the father was merely or primarily a masochistic attachment to the denying mother, whom he strove to displace in his creative work as artist. What he thought was a cause was an effect. In his ego he felt like an unclean pest, and it is to the dung beetle that his ego is reduced in "Metamorphosis."

. . . "Metamorphosis" is misleading as a title; it should be pluralized since the whole family constellation, father,

157

mother, and sister imagoes, are equally transformed in the
intrapsychic action. The drama as a whole is merely
activated by this upwelling into the conscious of the
infantile fantasy introject of the beloved and hated
maternal imago, which occurred when the hero was five
years of age. This initial conversion of the hero into the
image of the dung beetle is followed by the inward discharge or abreaction of the castration fantasy, with
progressive release, of the oral and anal fixations or
cathexes, until a total phallic libido is achieved, as symbolized in the three priapic gentlemen, the restoration of
the father and mother imagoes, and especially the nubility
of the emancipated anima, Grete. There is, obviously,
the symbolic death of the form into which the hero had
metamorphosed himself, but he resurrects in the re-
cathecting of the family constellation. Until Gregor as
beetle has abreacted the infantile, it is the picture of the
earth mother, with a fur cap on a fur stole, to which
he clings or by which he is possessed; but when all
metamorphoses are complete, and his infantile fixation has
been expiated, the mother-sister (or mother-daughter)
image is reinvested with phallic libido. Thereafter, the
officer projection [i.e. the projection of the ideal personality of Gregor in the teleological image of the officer in
military uniform] is the dominant, life-giving reality
within the psyche.

II

As "Metamorphosis" opens its intrapsychic action,
Gregor Samsa finds his ego world flooded by a volcanic
explosion of the repressed traumatic experience of the
terrible mother and the castrating father. He is, or
imagines himself to be, transformed into a huge beetle,
an object of consternation to himself, his family constellation, and his superego or employer. There is a curious
condensation of affect in the beetle: in one sense it is a
fantasy introject of the hated or castrating father, for it
is the father who attacks the son with the symbolic

apples; yet the energy impacted in the form of the beetle represents the amount of libido incestuously invested in the maternal imago, for it is the apple which is used for the symbolic castration, and it is the pre-oedipal (terrible) mother who appears at the end of the story to sweep out the remains of the desiccated beetle into which Gregor Samsa had been metamorphosed. In the concluding scene the father image achieves phallic identity through absorption and dominance of the three cigar-smoking gentlemen, and this genitalized libido transforms the violin-playing Grete into a marriageable young woman. . . .

The psychic problem of Gregor Samsa is to redeem through symbolic death that amount of libido impacted in incestuous longing for the mother's breast or womb and invested in patricidal destrudo. . . . The technique by which the pre-oedipal mother is released from her necessary and valuable psychic function of engulfing, strangling, or eating the infant who remains fixated on her breast seems stupidly cruel, and it is crude enough, but she is actually negatively redemptive since the terror she inspires as Sphinx forces the issues and the victim decides a little reluctantly that the possible terrors ahead are at least less obvious than those behind. Gregor's death as desiccated beetle and the disappearance (her work done) of the bony charwoman (with plume) are two elements in the pre-oedipal syndrome. Once this terrible phase of the Magna Mater has been energized and discharged (her work done), the benevolent, creative phase is activated; and the mother emerges in her duplicate Grete, who is sister, marriageable woman, and Virgin of Light. . . .

On one level of his being, Gregor Samsa had preferred his sister Grete to his mother, a more or less normal substitution and yet progression in the psychic evolution of the male. When the Chief Clerk arrives on the morning of the metamorphosis, Gregor was sure that if only his sister could have acted for him, the conflict would have been resolved. For Gregor has failed to catch the train

for work or psychic progression, and now the Chief Clerk
or superego is about to accuse him of sin. He has had a
peculiar love for this violin-playing sister, was fascinated
even to the end by her playing, and had even hoped to
provide for her musical education at the Conservatory.
. . . Yet on a deeper level, he is even more involved with
the picture he had cut out and framed, of the lady with
a fur cap and a fur stole. He would rather bite his dear
sister Grete than permit her to remove this picture from
his room. In fact, in most abject terror, he covers this
picture with his whole body as though embracing it in
defiance of all the members of his family constellation.
This Sphinx maternal imago is the antithesis of the marriageable Grete who appears as the action ends as the
prototype of the woman he will marry. The butcher boy
coming up the stairs with fresh supplies is the dream
symbol which guarantees that though deceased in his infantile form, the psyche as a whole is very much alive;
the libido formerly invested as incestuous toward the
mother and its concomitant patricidal destrudo are, in
fantasy, replaced by the new family constellation.

The castration fantasy thus resolved is a necessary, impersonal drive of the psyche toward wholeness or completion. A week before the actual metamorphosis or
reversion to the primary identification with the pre-
oedipal mother, Gregor had cut out of the magazine this
picture of the woman in furs and with his own precious
knife * had made the fretwork frame for it. This symbolic
castration appears in the cut finger, the white spots, the
wounded trailing foot, and finally in the splintered glass
and the corrosive liquid splashed on the face of Gregor
when his sister Grete tries to remedy his condition.
Grete is no less metamorphosed than Gregor, for instead
of remaining the spiritual twin or affinity of Gregor, it is
Grete who finally refers to the metamorphosed Gregor as
"It" and insists that unless he is disclaimed and rejected
the whole family will disintegrate. . . . The autoerotic

---

* This should, of course, be "fretsaw." [S.C.]

factor involved in the substitution of the sister for the
mother is transcended in the revitalization of both femi-
nine imagoes and the rejuvenescence of the father
image.

Grete as daughter fulfills the inner intention of the
mother, Mrs. Samsa, just as Persephone duplicated and
fulfilled the being of Demeter. Grete even assumes some
of the asthmatic symptoms of her mother, who is given to
choking for lack of breath, coughing hollowly into her
hand, and looking around with a wild expression in her
eyes. Such symptoms in the fantasy introject, of course,
indicate clearly enough the traumatic terror of the infant
denied the breast and projecting onto the mother image
his strangling rage with his own impotence. Accordingly,
when Grete comes into the room, she rushes to open the
window as though she too could not stand the fetid atmosphere, and it is Grete who insists on getting the
chest as symbolic womb out of the room (or psyche), or
since the representation is by reversal, getting Gregor as
beetle out of the womb. Later, when the witch mother
with broom and plume (the latter distressing even to Mr.
Samsa) has done her work, all the libido formerly invested
in her as destrudo is transformed and allocated to Grete,
who is now fully dressed, ready for work, without band
or collar. There is thus a psychic unity latent in the mother
in her consciously accepted form, the woman in furs as
infantile fantasy introject, the bony charwoman as pre-
oedipal, destroying mother, and the changing forms of
Grete. Such is a typical psychic progression of the anima
in man as we know it in the universal symbolism of myth
and dreams.

III

A more detailed analysis of the time and place elements in this fantasy of death and resurrection will clarify
the story. The hour-year analogue indicates that Gregor
should have caught the five o'clock train for work, that
is, a psychic change should have occurred at the normal

age of five, when the first awareness of a divided or sinful nature usually appears with the formation of the superego as accuser or inner conscience, in a confusing or distressing form. But here it is, already six-thirty (Gregor is six and a half years old); he has missed the train or psychic energy necessary for progression, and what is more he is unaccountably metamorphosed into a beetle. In fact, the alarm or inner monitor should have sounded at four, but something in the psyche failed to function, and now that he is ready to make the transitus from adolescence to maturity, the repressed fixation of the five-year old boy is activated, the conscious ego is invaded, and Gregor is reduced to the form of the denigrated maternal ego he had introjected as fantasy, probably while he was at his mother's breast. The woman in furs to which he is obsessively devoted is a variant of the cat or Sphinx mother, a constant archetype in all cultures.

As the topography shows, his personal room in this house, which represents the psyche as a whole, is his mother's womb. The chest and the writing table, over which so much anxiety develops, condense or concentrate this womb and the onanistic fantasies associated with such a fixation. To the left opens a door to a room occupied by his father and mother, or more correctly, his infantile fantasy introjects of these imagos. To the right or conscious, progressive side of his room, the life side, is the room occupied by his sister Grete, with whose dressing he is so much concerned because of its symbolic significance. There is a living room to the front, or Freudian preconscious, where there is traffic between the ego and the unconscious. The kitchen to the rear is the ordinary dream representation of the sources of the libido, where often enough women are preparing food for the renewal of the distressed ego, which is now under the flood or invasion of the basic fantasy introjects of the primary imagos, including the castrating father.

An acute sense of anxiety accompanies this metamorphosis; there will not be another train until seven o'clock. In the meantime, the porter will have informed the chief clerk that Gregor has not reported for work; and, sure enough, this representative of the employer or superego immediately arrives to investigate, to accuse, and to threaten. The father has not been able to work for five years; that is, the father has been psychically inactive as invigorating model or type, and the ego alone has been trying to run the household. What will become of this family constellation now that Gregor is reduced to the image of the destroying mother is of great concern. Not all of his father's original or potential capital has been lost; there is still some latent constructive energy in the paternal imago. Gregor, in fact, has been working to pay off his father's debts (or his debts to his father), unaware of this residual capital which does float the family through the misfortune which comes upon them through this metamorphosis of Gregor. The father image moves through the anality of the bank messenger (with his most precious uniform) to the point where it is he who orders the priapic gentlemen to clear out in order that he can take over. In other words, the endopsychic father image is metamorphosed as the original or prototype of Gregor himself. What happens to the father image is happening within the total psyche of Gregor. And likewise, the mother image moves through the successive forms of the Sphinx, the asthmatic mother who receives the smothered cry of the child, the charwoman, to the form in which she is cleansed and released into the expectation of a new life in better surroundings. And Grete is transformed from the onanistic fantasy into the marriageable young woman expectant of a husband.

The chief clerk arrives from his employer's office. . . . Gregor seems to be greatly concerned lest the chief clerk blame his parents for his failure to catch the five-o'clock train and begin to dun his parents for their unpaid debts, which, of course, are Gregor's or the equivalent of his failure to discharge his infantile fixation on the womb and his fear of his father, who must threaten castration in order to assist the ego into a mature appropriation of libido. The chief clerk implies that Gregor's absence may be due to the payment of certain sums of cash recently to Gregor. The last is the explanation of the debacle; cash represents here available libido to be reinvested in new, mature forms of the family constellation and the new adjustment of Gregor's ego. If there had been no resurgence of libido for a reconstructive effort, there would have been no metamorphosis. . . . Having done his work of convicting Gregor of psychic sin by forcing on him the condensed image of the denying mother and the denigrated father, the chief clerk leaves.

Naturally enough, within this intrapsychic action, the paternal image now takes over the symbolic phalli left by the chief clerk, or shall we say that conscience equips the father image with the necessary costume for his role as initiator and castrator: the walking stick, the hat, and the great cloak. As initiator the father now flourishes a newspaper threateningly, and hisses like a snake, driving Gregor back into his room. In real terror and self-pity, Gregor sees only the father who threatens castration, not knowing that upon completion of the psychic transformation, this same father will make the sign of the cross, with the women, over the defunct beetle.

This lex talionis is a requisite (in spite of the rational mind) for the redemptive or rebirth process. As the intrapsychic action intensifies, the hissing no longer sounds like that of a single father; the principle of masculinity becomes multitudinous and coercive. The father does not think of opening the other half of the door, and as the beetle is jammed in his retreat through it, his father bruises the traditional flank (displaced castration), and Gregor's blood flows freely, staining the white floor. As in the ancient mysteries and some forms of Christianity, without the shedding of blood there is no redemption. As the father closed the door with the stick, one of the beetle's little legs trailed uselessly behind him; the castration motif is complete, and the neophyte knows the terror and the pain of masochistic submission to the destroying mother and patricidal destrudo. It is a form of death inflicted as retaliation for a death willed in fantasy. . . .

IV

Interest is now distributed over the whole family constellation, for as in every reintegration process a dynamic shift of energy value at one point means a redistribution throughout the psyche. As Gregor awakens in the room he has occupied for five years, he smells the fresh bread and milk sops, and at first he is so pleased that he buries his head up to his eyes in the mess, much as he once nuzzled into his mother's breast. He is safe at least, and the object of great concern (like many a neurotic) to his family. It is his sister Grete who first looks into the room and finds the "beetle" hiding under the sofa. The curious masochistic desire to be denied, the price paid for oral aggression, is now manifested in Gregor's refusal of the fresh milk and his preference for old, decayed vegetables. . . .

As time passes, the hospital across the street, symbolic of the therapeutic process involved, is now beyond Gregor's range of vision; he might have believed that his window gave out onto a desert waste, a mere gray sky over a gray land. Imaginatively we are in the same realm as that in which Titorelli painted heathscapes in "The Trial," the waste land or the wilderness where rebirth alone can take place. Grete leaves an armchair by the window for her metamorphosed brother. There he has the appearance of a bogey, and a stranger might have thought that he was lying there in wait for his sister, intending to bite her. As his initial orientation to his sister had duplicated the infant's first dependence upon the benevolent mother, so now he duplicates the ambivalent reversal and attack upon the mother's breast, refusing her proffered food and ready to bite her. The curious breast-apple identity appears not only in the popular version of the Garden of Eden sin, but in the apples thrown by the father (lex talionis) into the back of the beetle Gregor. . . .

Hard times descend upon the household. Most important of all, a gigantic charwoman comes in to do the household work morning and evening. . . . Gregor's injustice collecting becomes complete as he sees his formerly loving sister pushing any old food toward him and leaving all manner of filth in his room. The anal libido even reverts upon his own metamorphosed body as it trails with filth along the floor. The bony charwoman, however, with her plume or phallus does not fear the pseudo-aggression of Gregor; she just commands him to come along now and threatens to bring a chair down on his head. But the split mother image remains partially protective and creative, for she cleans Gregor's room with several buckets of water. But Gregor is upset; the sister storms at the mother; and the father reprimands both mother and sister. Such is the intrapsychic confusion during the progressive phases of the rebirth process.

But at long last there appear the priapic deities as in the story "In the Penal Colony." These three gentlemen, symbolising the masculine genitals, now command the household, dominating the father, the mother, and the sister, until their authority is transferred to, or taken over by, the father himself. This is the climactic metamorphosis. As phallic entities they object to any vestigial analism; they have a special antipathy for dirt. . . . The bearded gentlemen are the form of libido in which he is to be resurrected, or would be, had Kafka chosen to complete the implied psychic action.

[At the conclusion of the story,] Gregor sees the breaking dawn through his window and quietly expires. This is the "Consummatum est": the infantile ego dominated by incestuous libido and patricidal destrudo is dead. . . . Mr. Samsa crosses himself, and his example is followed by the three women. The death of such a regressed, fixated libido, properly symbolized by a dung beetle, is indeed to be blessed if the psychic energy impacted in the form has already been channeled into the resurgent life of the other members of the family constellation. However grim the intrapsychic action of Kafka's stories, there are few in which the discerning reader does not see planted or suggested the abiding hope, the confirmed intention, of transcending his conflict and achieving wholeness.

With the curious condensation, representation by reversal, and transference characteristic of the dream, . . . Mr. Samsa now orders the three gentlemen out of the house, while he, in his splendid uniform, takes his wife on one arm and his daughter on the other. The phallic drive also has done its work. Gregor has become his own father; he is indeed metamorphosed. As the three gentlemen go down the stairs, they are metamorphosed into the butcher boy coming up the stairs with fresh supplies. Thus eros triumphs over thanatos. Since her morning's work is done, the charwoman is leaving. Mr. Samsa is still annoyed by the ostrich feather standing upright on her hat, for the mother of death is a most disturbing archetype in any psyche.

As they move on to the larger and fuller life, the members of Gregor Samsa's family constellation incorporate his own resurrected and transformed libido, and thus one of the most curious tales of death and resurrection is completed. From the very beginning of the action, Gregor was not only fixated in the depths of his being on the woman in furs; there was also that ideal portrait of himself, as a young officer, proud of his uniform and manly bearing, with his own God-given sword in his hand. Truly enough, the charwoman did dispose of the dead dung beetle, but the sword of Gregor disposed of the charwoman. The malignant mother has become the beloved sister, in the nuptial flight of her soul, ready for marriage. And, of course, the anima is the soul of man.

It seems, therefore, that though "Metamorphosis" is paradoxical because the dynamic transformation of libido does not center in the return or resurrection of the hero as centered in a new, absolute Self, Kafka has incorporated all the essential elements of the monomyth except this return. And this return is diffused into the family constellation, with the substitution of the reanimated and completely changed Grete (as anima) for the ego of the hero. We might say that Grete as anima or beloved is the psychic alternate which is resurrected or makes the return. It may be that Kafka could not project a completely redeemed ego because of the incommensurables existing between the old or artistic ego and the Self he wanted as man to be.

Peter Dow Webster, "Franz Kafka's 'Metamorphosis' as Death and Resurrection Fantasy." *American Imago*, XVI (1959). Pp. 349–65. Reprinted by permission of the editor, Dr. George B. Wilbur.

Walter H. Sokel

Education for Tragedy

The Metamorphosis . . . is the story of the traveling salesman Gregor Samsa, who wakes up one morning transformed into a monstrous vermin, retains his ability to think and feel as a human being, is held prisoner and hidden by his family, and slowly goes to his ruin. . . .

Gregor's spiritual situation in the family is duplicated exactly by the physical situation of his room. On the one hand he is surrounded, encircled, and closed in on all sides. Gregor, an adult, is a prisoner in his own family. . . . On the other hand, he is a total stranger in the family and lives in their midst in the state of exile which in his diary Kafka calls "Russian." His seclusion (*Abgeschlossenheit*) from the family is again shown, physically and literally, by his locking (*abschliessen*) the door of his room when he retires. When Gregor wakes up as a vermin, his main problem, since he has locked the door of his room the evening before, is reaching the others out of his literal seclusion. Kafka notes in his diary that his door was closed "in consideration of [his] age"; on the other hand his little nephew Felix slept with the door of his room wide open. "The open door indicated that they still wanted to lure Felix into the family while I was already excluded" (T240).*

Before the metamorphosis Gregor intended to send his younger sister to the Conservatory, even against the will of his parents, to whom he is otherwise obedient. . . . This mysterious event (the metamorphosis) makes it impossible, of course, for him to carry out his plan. Thus

---

* *Diaries, I,* 221. [S.C.]

the metamorphosis functions in one respect as a sentence in advance to prevent the son from arrogating paternal authority. That the father-son motif is crucial in *The Metamorphosis* Kafka confirmed by his plan to publish together the three stories from 1912, "The Judgment," *The Metamorphosis*, and "The Stoker," in a single volume, which was to have the title *The Sons* (See Br116). Of course the father-son motif is intimately linked with the motif of punishment and condemnation. Kafka's later plan was to publish "The Judgment," *The Metamorphosis*, and "In the Penal Colony" in a book to be entitled *Punishments*.

The immediate function of the metamorphosis, then, is to prevent an imminent rebellion of the son . . . and to put to an end the reversal of the natural relation between father and son. Through Gregor's metamorphosis, the father becomes masterful again and reasserts himself as head of the family. Thus *The Metamorphosis* is the resurrection and rejuvenation of a father held to be senile. The son, for his part, sinks into a dreadful state, which far exceeds the degradation of senility. . . .

In *The Metamorphosis* the struggle for power and the desire for flight are fused in the single figure of Gregor Samsa. The structural principle of the story is thus self-division.* Self-division takes actual form when the mentality of a young, conscientious traveling salesman is imprisoned in the body of a gigantic vermin. With the metamorphosis, a principle of alienation, the "pure self" [working in implicit alliance with the father] takes possession of Gregor, automatically topples the usurpatory son from his position of power in the family, and returns the father to his former rank.

But besides toppling the son, the metamorphosis has two other, quite different functions. It represents dissatis-

---

* Benno von Wiese calls attention to the divided consciousness in *The Metamorphosis*. The metamorphosis is an existential crisis and evidently points to "a split between conscious and unconscious" (von Wiese, 330–331).

faction and, at the same time, its opposite, the longing for the restoration in the family of the warm and harmonious relations which have vanished. Before elucidating these three aspects of *The Metamorphosis*, we want to define more precisely the "pure self" by tracing back the image of the bug or beetle in Kafka's work.

The image of the beetle first appears in "Wedding Preparations in the Country," an unfinished youthful novel of Kafka's which, according to Max Brod, dates from the years 1907 and 1908, thus four to five years before the composition of *The Metamorphosis*. The hero of the novel, a young man named Rabin—the number and arrangement of the letters prefigures the name Samsa, which is, however, still more like Kafka than Raban was *—enjoys imagining that in order to avoid exertion and discomfort, he splits his self. His authentic self stays home in the form of a gigantic beetle resting in bed. His "clothed body," literally his façade, staggers out into the world to do the job.

The beetle appears here as the symbol of the "pure" self. This self is inhuman. It has voluntarily divested itself of human form. Indeed, it has not even turned into a mammal and vertebrate but into an insect; thus it is as remote as possible from man, as Kafka once saw himself in his diary: "And I have become cold again, and insensible. . . . And like some kind of beast at the farthest pole from man, I shift my neck from side to side again" (T444).† It is celibate; indeed the desire for celibacy is the reason why, after all, it constitutes itself as a pure self and accomplishes the division. Its deepest wish is not to be burdened with women. But here women represent life, the world, society, and humanity in general. This self lies in complete repose on its bed in the silent room, in deep and mystic harmony with itself. But it is also connected to the external world in a magical

---

* Charles Neider has called attention to the cryptogram of Kafka in the name Samsa.

† *Diaries, II*, 98. [S.C.]

way. While the self dreams, it is omnipotent. It has absolute control over the men and cars in front of the windows. Every movement they make they must ask as a favor from the huge, resting beetle by looking at him. But he does not put any obstacle in their way. Between him and mankind there exists a harmonious, paradisiacal relation, a total contentment. Precisely in excluding himself, precisely in his inhumanity and retirement (*Abgeschiedenheit*—the word Kafka uses in his diary), he has become the heart of mankind.

How "pathetic" on the other hand is his façade self, which must toil in the outside world. It staggers around in the world and is restless while the beetle rests. It sobs while the beetle dreams. Its position in life is exactly that of Gregor Samsa, the traveling salesman, before his metamorphosis, and is therefore imperfect, unsteady, tormented, and "void." Its relation to the world is that of struggle and strategy. Therefore it is pathetic, powerless —precisely, "human."

On the other hand, the beetle Raban, his true self, attains through metamorphosis and self-division absolute "calm." This marvelous condition of being entirely at home with oneself is simultaneously a being wholly connected with the world—without struggle, without fragmentation, without conflict and without, of course, actual human contact. It is a condition of "retirement" of the soul, not unlike the condition which all mysticism seeks. As in Indian mysticism, submersion in the self is also "submersion in the *atman*," unification with the *atman* of the cosmos, the breath of the world. Here, the "draft" which blows through Raban's room is noteworthy. At the primordial basis of the soul we are also at the basis of being.

The two beetle metamorphoses in Kafka's work have this in common: they represent a tendency to retire, to retreat, from the world, and at the same time the opposite: the attempt to dominate the world through magical parasitism and to claim for oneself a state of emergency which frees the self from all effort and responsibility.

Thus in both cases the metamorphosis is the unification of an opposition. It is at once abdication and pretension, withdrawal and aggression. The difference is only that Raban longs for his metamorphosis as his fulfillment, while for Gregor Samsa this fulfillment always remains unconscious. Gregor can never accept with his consciousness the wishful element in the metamorphosis. And so precisely the element which characterizes the condition of the "beautiful" beetle Raban—the mystic peace of retirement, the *raison d'être* of his dehumanization—is forever denied to the odious vermin Gregor Samsa. His conscience gives him no peace. He must endure the deepest thing in himself as a catastrophe which breaks in on him from the outside, as something merely awkward, not as the wish fulfillment which the metamorphosis represents for Raban. Consequently Raban is a beautiful beetle, but Samsa a disgusting, repugnant "vermin." * However, in the actual structural function which the metamorphosis has in the story, elements are revealed which run completely counter to Gregor's consciousness.

In its practical result the metamorphosis represents Gregor's refusal to toil any further for the family. With the metamorphosis he gives up his façade self, that of the overworked traveling salesman, and lets a deeper concealed tendency in himself come to light. He withdraws —unconsciously, certainly—into the lap of idleness and lets the others take care of themselves. The metamorphosis functions in its practical result as the flight from responsibility, work, and duty.

---

* To Emrich the beetle embodies the self beyond ideas of itself. "The animal is the absolute disaffirmation of the so-called 'human' world, although it is nothing but man 'himself.' The split between 'having ideas' and 'being' (Emrich, Ger. edition, p. 127; *131*). According to Emrich, Raban sees the world from the standpoint of the immovable resting self, from the standpoint of the truth, and therefore the world must seem to him loathsome and perverted. On the other hand, Samsa wants to remain in the world, and therefore the resting self seems to him a horrible monster.

In contrast with "The Judgment," *The Metamorphosis* is a self-inflicted punishment, which is at the same time a rebellion or, better, a "strike"; and so here punishment and fresh guilt are strangely mixed with one another.

Gregor's interior monologue at the outset of the metamorphosis reveals that for a long time he has harbored deep feelings of aversion and dissatisfaction toward his job. He found his life as a traveling salesman acutely uncomfortable and inhumanly harassed, like the pitiful staggering of Raban's façade self. He would have given up his position a long time ago if his father had not been in debt to the head of the firm, forcing Gregor to slave until the debt was paid off.

Already we see the second function of the metamorphosis define itself. The metamorphosis releases Gregor from having to drudge any further. If the metamorphosis has really "transformed" him, he thinks, he cannot be "required" any more to go on slaving. He will be at once excused and exculpated, that is, freed from guilt and debt (*"ent-schuldigt"*). Seen this way, the metamorphosis is "exculpated" insubordination—not open rebellion, but a flight into shirking, an act which must have even direr consequences for the family than an open refusal to serve. In a single blow the family loses its breadwinner. Yet Gregor is at the same time "exculpated": he is not responsible for the event.

A psychosomatic sickness would have served the same purpose. We remember that Kafka himself felt the discovery of his tuberculosis to be a liberation. At the beginning of *The Metamorphosis* sickness is mentioned several times.* Gregor himself thinks he may have a "cold" and recalls not having felt well the evening before. His mother wants to call the doctor. But all these allusions and associations are dropped once and for all as soon as Gregor appears in the door of the living room. There is no further talk linking the metamorphosis with sickness. Why?

---

* Benno von Wiese stresses the analogy between metamorphosis and sickness (330).

Gregor is treated neither as an ordinary vermin nor as a human being, son, and brother, but as the embodiment of the most disgusting and dangerous side of his personality, without the tinge of anything better, purer, or more human.

This is because the metamorphosis fulfills a function which sickness could not fulfill. It comes forth as terrible aggression. It turns Gregor into a thing whose mere appearance strikes anxiety and terror into people or else goads them, as it does the father, into rage. That is the side of the metamorphosis—aggression—unconsciously embodying Gregor's bitter discontent.

The other side of the metamorphosis is helplessness. As aggression, the metamorphosis represents guilt, an indebtedness which Gregor feels often enough, precisely because it is a cowardly "exculpation" and his surrogate for open rebellion. As helplessness, on the other hand, it represents a self-disarming and punishment for the guilt. No temporal sequence is present here. We might think of Dante's *Inferno*, in which punishment is the eternal embodiment of sin. The sinner becomes his sin: this is his punishment. And so Gregor Samsa has become his revenge, his desire to exploit others, his parasitism—and this is his punishment. His ambivalence, his self in permanent division, have taken concrete form. Guilt and punishment united in one body and incarnated, in every act and every movement of his body, as contradictory, divided unity—this is Gregor's fate!

The most striking instances [of Gregor's hopeless division] occur, significantly, at the moment when he first shows himself in his metamorphosed shape to the others. His body commits two aggressive acts which his consciousness knows nothing of. As he enters the living room he snaps (*schnappt*) his jaws several times in the air. His mother, who has just recovered from her first shock, is once again terrified. The actual act of Gregor's body, the "snapping," expresses voracity, menace, bestiality. And yet Gregor's intentions aim at communicating with his mother, at restoring loving intimacy with her. At the level of consciousness Gregor is the tender son, man seeking contact and love. At a more fundamental level of his being, over which his consciousness exercises no control ("he could not resist snapping his jaws"), he is nothing but violent greed; he snatches (*schnappt*) at his share of the goods of the table and of life, from which he has been excluded by the others and by himself. This level, which is diametrically opposed to consciousness, is by far the stronger and more essential; and it is the only one which manifests itself for the others. His tender, benevolent, human consciousness has been so repressed that it cannot manifest itself anymore. The expression ("he could not resist") is characteristic. In it is revealed the dimension in the metamorphosis of anarchy, remonstration, undiscipline, the flight into irresponsibility and licentiousness, parasitism. The dynamism of self-division which is the metamorphosis becomes even more clearly visible in Gregor's behavior toward the office manager. Even before the metamorphosis Gregor harbored strong feelings of revenge against the hated boss. He wanted to topple him from his position of authority but unfortunately had to postpone this aggressive act on account of his parents. Now the metamorphosis becomes a weapon of gruesome aggression against the boss's emissary. At the sight of Gregor he retreats, terrified.

•   •   •

Gregor's internal contradiction between conscious intention and unintentional occurrence is comparable to the "accidental act" (*Fehlleistung*) [as anatomized by Freud]. Accidental acts originate in closest proximity to jokes [a diversion of unconscious aggression into purgative laughter]. However, by the very fact of their being acts, they might quite easily result in tragic consequences. In his conscious intent Gregor wants to be, and is, the supplicant. But in fact he appears as a persecutor and acts as an aggressor. His inaudible words plead, his visible gestures threaten. Between consciousness and fact a contradiction yawns, expressing the split between consciousness and body, self and world.

•   •   •

Gregor actually wants to realize his aggressive and [as we shall see] his erotic daydreams. [In his wish to keep his sister sequestered] the desire for incest emerges alongside of resentment. But this desire is not love, it is aggression. Gregor's dream of an idyll with his sister is dominated by egoism, the drive for power, aggressivity, and self-admiration. Not the enchanted prince, who pleads to be recognized, but the dragon who guards his trove, links Gregor's wish fulfillment with fairy tale and myth. The thing that distinguishes *The Metamorphosis* from the fairy tale is not only the fact, as Heselhaus believes, that Gregor is not "recognized" by his world, but that for him love as an uninterrupted feeling is impossible. The destiny he intends for his sister would be dreadful. In an empty room, a cave, she would be abandoned to the caresses of a garbage-bedraggled vermin. Dante could have conceived this image as a punishment for incest.

•   •   •

We find in *The Metamorphosis* the archetypal eroticism of Kafka's work. The love relation to the woman is first and foremost a weapon in the struggle of the hero with the wielder of power. The woman is also bait, a tool for bribery and influence, for putting the authority in a more favorable disposition. Thus Gregor would have been glad to use his sister as confederate and bait to influence the office manager.

•   •   •

The erotic sphere serves the strategy of the hero in his struggle for self-assertion and recognition by the author-

ity. In *The Metamorphosis* the woman is also a weapon
used directly and aggressively against the prototype of
the wielder of power in Kafka's work, the father. The
wishdream in which Gregor uses his "terrifying appearance" to come forth as the dragon who protects the prin-
cess in his cave is basically a declaration of war against
the father. . . . Here Gregor repeats in his thoughts the
project which he has already conceived once before the
metamorphosis and which the metamorphosis has prevented: that of tearing his sister away from his father.
But now the metamorphosis has grown false to its original
function, which was precisely supposed to prevent this
project, and threatens to turn into the opposite of its
original intent.

Gregor wants the best of both worlds. He wants to fuse
the mystic and unearthly inwardness of Raban, the "unknown nourishment" which seems to offer itself to him
in the violin playing of his sister, with the world of the
façade self, of sensual gratification, human intimacy, and
masculine power. Gregor wants the impossible. This
comes to light in the monstrous fairy-tale quality of his
daydream. The hubris of the pure self manifests itself.
Gregor puffs himself up with pride at his exceptional status, turns his misfortune into a sign of election, and
arrogantly looks down on common men who chew earthly
nourishment with their teeth. . . . Precisely in this passage Kafka's style becomes sentimental and monstrously
subjective. One has only to think of Gregor's kisses on
Grete's neck; and how can he "confide" anything to his
sister, who for months has not been able to hear or understand him? Deliberately, the style becomes captive of
the kitsch with which it expresses the parodic and tragic-
ironic dimension of Gregor's wishdream.

It is his sister who in a cruel and ironic reply to Gregor's
"subjective" dream, in a tone hard, simple, and direct,
shows him the way back to the original destiny of the
metamorphosis.

"It has to go," cried his sister. "That's the only answer,

Father. You just have to try to get rid of the idea that it's Gregor. Believing it for so long, that is our real misfortune. But how can it be Gregor? If it were Gregor, he would have realized long ago that it isn't possible for human beings to live with such a creature, and he would have gone away of his own free will. Then we wouldn't have a brother, but we'd be able to go on living and honor his memory."

"If it were Gregor, he would have gone away of his own free will." With this the innermost meaning of the metamorphosis becomes clear. Gregor's authentic self is death. Gregor himself now sees this and fully agrees with his sister. "His conviction that he would have to disappear was, if possible, even firmer than his sister's." With this thought, this certainty, he finds inner peace and "contentedly" surrenders to death.

Characteristically, his sister accepts the metamorphosis as an empirical fact, as something which certainly could have happened to her brother. The "miracle" of the metamorphosis itself is not put into question, but only its interpretation. Only Gregor's behavior toward the metamorphosis is discussable. And now it becomes evident that Gregor has a genuine and tragic choice. He can turn false to his fate and betray himself by insisting, despite the metamorphosis, which summons him to something quite different, on the rights of his body and person—and in this way first turn into a monster. For it is only when the "calm" beetle, who as pure seclusion and interiority is dehumanized, brings into his metamorphosis the lusts of the carnal man, that he turns into vermin. But he can also faithfully follow his summons, the inner significance of the metamorphosis, and "go"—that is, grasp that it is his destiny to withdraw from the world, to redeem the world from himself, and only by so doing be "honored."

The right interpretation of the metamorphosis would thus be Gregor's "going." It is to this that the miracle of his destiny summons him. So Gregor himself understands it at the end of his sufferings. Death is the meaning of his existence—this is what the metamorphosis is supposed to teach him. . . .* Not like Raban's dream, as self-delight, but as tragic sacrifice, the metamorphosis becomes the meaning of Gregor's existence.

Gregor's metamorphosis is sacrifice. A former state of harmony profoundly disturbed and wrenched by the father's "debt" or "guilt" is restored through the sacrifice of the son. Five years before the metamorphosis the father's business failure had plunged the family into grave difficulties. Then Gregor had begun to work "with special passion." Then, for the first time, Gregor took over the "debt" or "guilt" of the family. At first this led to "wonderful times" of love, warmth and harmony, but thereafter to the gradual usurpation of the father's role by the son, now sole breadwinner and family support. This was no salvation, only a deeper entanglement.

•   •   •

With the metamorphosis Gregor takes the "debt" upon himself for the second time. The metamorphosis provides him with the possibility of abdication, of freedom from the struggle and from earthly entanglements. The innermost meaning of the metamorphosis is Gregor's death, so that the family, freed from his false role, can live again.

But the metamorphosis was from the beginning two-faced and ambiguous. It was not only sacrifice for the family but also the opposite—sacrifice of the family. It was not only abdication but also pretension, not only contentment but discontent, not only inwardness and retreat into the pure self but aggression and eruption as a "terrifying figure." Above all, a new hubris showed itself in it, which came to ghastly fruition just after Gregor was wounded by his father: this was Gregor's dream of incest in the

---

* Landsberg sees in *The Metamorphosis* the desire to return to the inorganic state and conceives Gregor's metamorphosed condition as an existence bound up with death (Landsberg, 122–33). Benno von Wiese also sees that the metamorphosis tends toward death (von Wiese, 343–44).

ivory tower, of *splendid isolation*,* of fairy-tale happiness.

•   •   •

Instead of liberating the family, the metamorphosis topples them into still greater weakness, disgrace, contemptible misery. Characteristic of this is the grotesque and pathetic role which the father has to play *vis à vis* the roomers. What a fall. . . . As once before, Gregor's sacrifice is of no use. In the fall of the father figure the metamorphosis which at first rejuvenated and strengthened him appears to have lost its purpose: neither Gregor nor the family have been redeemed; the curse, the "debt," is only multiplied and increased. Gregor's self-sacrifice has once again had the opposite effect from that toward which it was first moving.

But with the catastrophe, the cruel truth-revealing outcry of his sister, understanding of the tragic meaning of his metamorphosis dawns on Gregor. Gregor dies reconciled: he still glimpses the morning, the light of the beginning day. But with his death the family regains, as if at one blow, its former dignity. . . . Salvation is at hand. The "indebted" or "inculpated" family is exculpated, returned to life. . . . On past Gregor's corpse, through his death, his disapperance, life blooms anew —redeemed, ready to engender new life in place of the old life gone astray, entangled in guilt. Here is the structure of authentic tragedy. . . . †

The objection has been raised ‡ that this Samsa family

---

* In English in the original. [S.C.]

† Benno von Wiese very rightly compares the end of *The Metamorphosis* with the end of *The Hunger Artist*. Grete Samsa embodies the same cruel triumph of vitality over the hero which the leopard, admired by the public, represents in the cage of the dead hunger artist. See, too, Meno Spann's "Franz Kafka's Leopard," *The Germanic Review*, XXXIV (1959), pp. 85–104. [Also see notes *100–01*. S.C.]

‡ For example, by Heselhaus, who characterizes *The Metamorphosis* as an anti-fairy tale, as a description of the world "as it should not be."

is so horrible that its salvation and its continuance form
the genuine tragedy of the work and that therefore
Gregor's sacrifice is wholly senseless, mere confirmation
of the paradoxical absurdity of existence. This objection
overlooks the fact that Kafka, precisely by showing the
triviality and, in every sense of the word, "common"
quality of life, without the camouflage of ideal or idyll,
truly intensifies the pain that lies in all tragedy. Life
is as "common" as the Samsa family, and it is precisely
such commonness that the death of the individual must
serve. The hatred with which Kafka sees this family (and
his own family in his diaries and letters) must not con-
ceal the more profound ambivalence with which, on the
other hand, he saw the family, the community, the
"stream of life" without sentimental idealization as in-
finitely superior to the individual. Precisely in this lies
the sharpness and distinctiveness of Kafka's tragedy—in
this terrible objectivity, with which what is positive and
victorious is robbed of the ornament of beauty and sub-
limity, indeed even of the cothurnus of justice.

The Metamorphosis is a tragedy constructed not on the
structural principle of realism, but on the principles of
the dream life. The metamorphosis itself is, by logical and
empirical laws, absurd. It is precisely not a fact become
symbol but a symbol become fact. But there are other
"magical" contradictions and absurdities, too, which can
only be understood by the logic of the dream, where what
is undescribable becomes event. This is customarily over-
looked, and the *realism* of the story (once the one "miracle" of the metamorphosis has been accepted) is praised.

But what, for example, has happened to the "debt"
with which the chain of events began? Gregor was far
from having paid off his parents' debt to the boss, and
for this reason had to postpone for years his rebellion to
gain his freedom. After his metamorphosis we hear nothing further about this debt. What has happened? Was it
paid off?

·   ·   ·

These would be concerns of a realistic author, in whose work fact must be symbol. But in Kafka's work, as in the dream, the symbol is the fact. A world of pure significance, of sheer expression, is represented deceptively as a sequence of empirical facts. . . . The fact is there only for the sake of its meaning.

For this reason we do not hear anything more about the "debt." The "debt" or "guilt" was precisely Gregor himself. He had taken it upon himself, and through the metamorphosis he has become it. The "debt" of the family has embodied itself in his terrifying figure, has passed over from the family into him. His metamorphosis was the liberation of the family from the debt. The office manager is driven away by Gregor and never returns. Yet the debt now continues to exist in Gregor's "repulsive shape" as a brandmark become visible. It is only with his physical disappearance that the memory of the debt is also extirpated, and a new apartment can be rented in which nothing will be left over from the epoch of the debt. With this the "wonderful times" return which Gregor could remember—but without him. Through his disappearance they return.

Gregor's death is not only a sacrifice, but also his deepest fulfillment, which, in tragic irony, falls to his lot. Behind and below its aggression the metamorphosis had the opposite function. It was a display of helplessness. Gregor's debasement and inoffensiveness were supposed to make it possible for the family to accept him again and to have "wonderful times" once more. Through his unintended usurpation of the dominant position in the family, Gregor had not been able to rekindle the old warmth. Coldness and lack of feeling, mere cohabitation and the joyless performance of duty had, on Gregor's part, replaced the old harmony. But with his "innocent" abdication following his metamorphosis, Gregor has demonstrated his inoffensiveness, and now like a child asks to be taken back into the intimate circle.

•   •   •

In each of his three advances and attempted escapes, his motivation was always that of achieving connection with the family, of breaking through the isolation which had begun long before the metamorphosis, and of being recognized. But the result was always the paradoxical reversal, the exact opposite of the intention: a kick and imprisonment, an injury which almost cost him his life, and finally expulsion and a death sentence.

At its most profound level the metamorphosis is more than abdication and a display of helplessness. It is a plea for help, a "prayer" for reconciliation, as writing was for Kafka, an entreaty that the barriers be torn down which had arisen between Gregor and the family ever since he had assumed the position of power. At the very beginning of the metamorphosis Gregor hopes, although he naturally cannot trust his hope, that his father will help him get out of bed. And in each of his encounters with his father this is his sole motive: to be understood by his father, to submit to his father's will, in no way, even at the cost of his life, to cross him. Gregor would rather suffer the violence of the "blow" from his father's boot "which was truly his salvation" than insist on freedom and the rights of his own person. By putting his total helplessness on display, he aims at reconciliation. Above all, his metamorphosis signifies that he has to stay home in a condition of the closest spatial contact with his family. Nothing means more to him than contact with them. He eavesdrops at the locked door and again and again attempts from his darkness to snatch glances into the circle of light out there. There is no more trenchant definition of the meaning of the story than Kafka's suggestion for an illustration for *The Metamorphosis:* the longing of the outcast for the inner circle, of the prodigal son for the family that has cast him out, of the man banished into darkness for the light—a light that is, however, nothing nobler, loftier, or more sacred than a lamp which shines on a group of petit-bourgeois, truly heartless human beings.

It is, however, Gregor's destiny to be reconciled with his family through his death and not through his life with the group. This was his role from the moment that he took upon himself the "debt" of his parents. What constitutes Gregor's authentic self is not flight into the pure self but the attainment once again of the harmony and happiness of childhood and boyhood. His deepest wish is not, like Raban, to rest sufficient unto himself in solitary peace, but rather to see the family blossom once again, and with them and in them, not outside them and without them, to blossom himself. His last thought is devoted to his family in "deep emotion and love." Intimately united with them in death as once before only in childhood and boyhood, he dies peacefully, fulfilled not by mystical self-immersion but by amiability and "ease." The "nourishment" for which Gregor longed remained "unknown" to him as long as, like a rapacious monster, he sought it in garbage and cheese parings and as long, too, as he hoped to find it by means of the pure self, as hunger artist, music connoisseur, and egocentric decadent.

Gregor Samsa's authentic destiny was to be tragic and not "sacred," and it was the role of the sister to make that clear to him. He must come to know that life does not need him or rather, that he is needed as redeemer, who redeems life by redeeming it of himself, of "guilt." * No Christ, but a tragic hero—and one of the most tragic in world literature, because he must remain deprived of human dignity, the "beautiful form" of the human shape. Gregor's reward is a wholly inward one.

"The Judgment" and *The Metamorphosis* are works of the very greatest significance for Kafka's entire oeuvre. Not only did he find in them his structural form, classical

---

* In Kafka's letter to Max Brod of July, 1922, the writer is defined as "the scapegoat of humanity." The writer "is the scapegoat of mankind, he allows men to enjoy a sin innocently, almost innocently" (Br 386). This definition of the writer in his relation to mankind fits exactly Gregor's relation to his family. The analogy noted by Politzer (77) of the names Gregor and Gregorius, the hero of the medieval epic of Hartmann von Aue, might be mentioned in this connection. Through hideous punishment and exposure Gregorius is indeed metamorphosed from incestuous stain on mankind to its saint and intercessor.

Expressionism, but all his themes are also contained in them *in nuce*. Here Kafka's myth attained its first valid and perfect form.

"Die Erziehung zur Tragik." From Walter H. Sokel, *Franz Kafka: Tragik und Ironie*. Munich and Vienna: Albert Langen, Georg Müller, 1964. Pp. 77–103. [Trans. S.C.] By permission of the publisher. Copyright © 1964 by Albert Langen Georg Müller Verlag GmbH, Munich and Vienna.

Friedrich Beissner

The Writer Franz Kafka

The epilogue to *The Metamorphosis*—told from the perspective of Gregor Samsa's parents and sister—is longer by around five pages [than the epilogue to "The Judgment"]. On the other hand, from its first sentence *The Metamorphosis* looks in onto the dreamlike, distorted loneliness of the sick hero who imagines he has turned into a monstrous vermin. Not for a moment does the narrator depart from this intimate connection at the interior of the hero's subjectivity. For the narrator, and consequently for the reader, Gregor *is* transformed into a monstrous bug. It would be wholly impossible for the writer even to intimate that this metamorphosis is only a delusion of the sick hero: in so doing he would destroy the specific density of his story.

But can we be certain that this is the case? Look: I have here a copy of the first printing (1916).* On the cover is a drawing (by Ottomar Starke) done presumably not without the author's consent, very probably even with his cooperation or at his request. You see a man in a dressing gown and slippers, who desperately throws up his hands in front of his face and moves with a long stride into the center of the room toward the spectator away from the opened door, which is not open for him; for outside is—do you see the black?—outside is darkness, nothingness. The man can only be Gregor Samsa himself, not, say, his elderly father. That is proved by the dark hair and the youthful vigor of the movement of the striding figure. This then *is* Gregor Samsa, the Gregor Samsa who

---

* Actually, November, 1915. [S.C.]

in the first sentence of the story was already transformed into a monstrous bug. You understand too: Kafka the artist could allow himself this hint outside the work of art. In the story itself there was no possibility for it.

From Friedrich Beissner, *Der Erzähler Franz Kafka.* Stuttgart: Kohlhammer, 1952. Pp. 36–37. [Trans. S.C.] By permission of the publisher.

Friedrich Beissner

Kafka the Poet

On May 10, 1953, the creator of that cover drawing, the illustrator Ottomar Starke, wrote in the *Neue literarische Welt* that he had not known Kafka personally and had not acceded to any request on his part concerning the illustration.

With this, however, I do not think that the conjecture asserted in the passage above is refuted. For I have said only that the drawing was "done presumably not without the author's consent, very probably even with his cooperation or at his request." Is it conceivable that no draft of the cover had been submitted to the author for his approval? His "request," too, his suggestion (before the commission was given to Starke) can have gone quite the same route as his consent afterward, namely to the publisher. It is known how much Kurt Wolff respected Kafka. This is evidenced by his letter of November 3, 1921, which Max Brod passes on in his biography and in which there is the sentence: "From the bottom of my heart may I assure you that I personally have so strong a feeling for you and your work as I only have in the case of two or perhaps at most three of the writers whom we represent, and whom we are permitted to bring before the public." *

. . . And so is it conceivable that a publisher who evidently respected his author so highly should have been so indifferent to the illustration of *The Metamorphosis* that he would have left it entirely to the discretion of the illustrator who at that time was apparently still very

---

* Franz Kafka, *Eine Biographie*, New York, 1946. P. 167.

young? (Starke speaks in 1953 in his article of his "nearly
forty years' practice," and the drawing was done in 1915,
thus thirty-eight years before.) And so [it stands to
reason] Wolff will have made a suggestion at the time of
commissioning [the drawing]—a matter which of course
Starke will hardly still be able to remember—in agreement
with Kafka or entirely on his own.

Now in the meantime Starke has evidently read a lot
about Kafka, and it makes him uneasy that his early work
is being "adduced as the criterion of an interpretation of
Kafka" which runs counter to the rest. For this reason
he now informs us of the commission of "an illustrated
title page" which consists in "condensing the content of
a book into a sort of catch-word. The catch-word for
Kafka's *The Metamorphosis* was: Horror! Despair! . . .
The figure fleeing in terror has black hair because the
head is black on white, thus, for pictorial reasons, and if
he wears dressing gown and slippers, then that is to show
the irruption of a very 'non-bourgeois' catastrophe into a
very 'humdrum bourgeois' existence."

If I understand Starke correctly, he means to say that
the male figure drawn by him at no point appears in the
story. I am afraid that here his memory is deceiving him.
Yet what is one supposed to make of the assertion that
the male figure has black hair only "for pictorial reasons"?
One may scarcely assert the more plausible explanation,
so obvious is it: it is not that the hair is black because
the background is white, but the background is white because the hair is black, the hair of the foreground figure,
which is after all the real and sole object of the illustration. The dark cross-hatching of the wall to the right of the
door also does not seem to indicate only the shadow cast
by the open wing of the door (which, moreover, doesn't
really tally with the shadow of the male figure); for the
wall is also done in black to the left and above the door
where there is no shadow. Yet the cross-hatching stops
where the black hair of the figure who already exists is
supposed to stand out starkly—"for pictorial reasons"!

COMMENTARY

[Binion, who considers Beissner's interpretation fruitful, writes, "Even so the evidence would be equivocal at best: Gregor reminisces much, and the scene may be one prior to his illness. Furthermore, some of the details do not fit the tale, however construed. On the other hand, the tale does afford full *internal* evidence that Kafka meant Gregor's illness as mental and not physical" (214–15).

For a further contribution to this discussion, see Henel, as well as Kafka's letter to Wolff of October 25, 1915.

From Friedrich Beissner, *Kafka der Dichter*. Stuttgart: Kohlhammer, 1958. Pp. 40–42. [Trans. S.C.] By permission of the publisher.

Helmut Richter

"The Metamorphosis"

The Metamorphosis depicts a failure which leads to death. . . . Gregor feels that because his job stultifies him as a human being, he cannot continue working any longer and in a moment of natural weakness is ruined. And so Kafka does not really depict a failure arising from human inferiority but a man's going to pieces from the consequences of his working life on his private existence as a human being. Gregor is a salesman whose job demands an all-out effort from him. . . . Let a man want the best for his family and devote himself completely to his job, and it can happen that as a result the life of the family itself is destroyed, because the human element must withdraw. Let a man, on the other hand, be reluctant to sacrifice completely to his livelihood his life as a human being, and this can lead to his neglecting his natural duty of assuring his family a decent living.

The problematical life of Kafka's heroes is rooted in the profound danger to humanity of the demands of bourgeois acquisitive life, which under imperialism grow more and more intense and lead to greater and greater contradictions in the life not only of society but of each individual family. The demand that a man do his duty under all circumstances, that he satisfy both the human and social claims on him, remains abstract as long as it fails to take into account the latent opposition of men to the forms and laws of everyday bourgeois life. And so Gregor's capitulation to the exhausting working conditions of his job cannot amount to an automatic proof of his inferiority and unfitness for life. . . . But the content of Kafka's theses is doubtless just this negative appraisal, even when he puts it into question by his clear-cut sympathy for his unfortunate heroes, and invites, by the tragic character of the dénouement, not only pity but reflection. The incongruity of Gregor's fate—an incongruity which the reader feels in view of the mercilessness of his sentence—suggests the objective conditions which cause him to become guilty, but which are suppressed in Kafka by the intensity with which he ascribes to his heroes a fundamental inhumanity and inferiority. The rigor of this conception, whose ultimate causes probably become intelligible only in light of the writer's biography, could not prevent him, however, from bringing more or less clearly to light the objective conditions of their disaster. As a result the impression cannot arise that his stories reflect only abnormalities. They depict in a willful form the very real distress of men who in the face of hard conditions of work and life search desperately for the right way. Their effort is desperate because there does not appear to be for them any life forms other than the bourgeois, because they do not recognize that these forms must necessarily collide with the claims of a truly human way of life. From the same bourgeois standpoint Kafka can see in his figures only unnatural exceptions, who have not fulfilled the human norm and have thus condemned themselves to solitude and to death.

The Metamorphosis stands close to the line where the aesthetic reflection of meaningful human reality stops and the simple illustration of conceptual systems and dogmas begins; these have been, to be sure, intensively experienced and structured but they are hardly able to contain an essential and valid statement. . . . Kafka's interest was always in the individual problem of the hero intensified to the extreme, while the conditioning social environment was illuminated by only a few—of course, frequently significant—reflexes [*sic*]. Kafka portrays human beings who have a fragile relation to the world around them; he brings this to light at an aesthetically pregnant juncture, then develops the conflict continuously until the catastrophe. He does not consider whether and to what extent this situation is influenced by contradictions in reality, since he is bent on explaining all antitheses and catastrophes by means of the anomalousness and weakness of his heroes, when he is not, as in *Description of a Struggle,* declaring inhumanity and chaos to be the nature of the world, and in so doing once again obstructing from view the crucial realities.

Thus the question arises: What meaning and what possibilities can the life of men have who are unable to find any connection with bourgeois reality? Kafka did not know a way out for them, for he saw only the given bourgeois life and its life forms. He could only confirm of his heroes that they had struggled with the best will in the world to cope with this life, before succumbing, and through the tragic configuration of their destiny, which appears to protest against life itself, testify to his sincere sympathy for them. And in this perhaps lies the beginning of a revision of his ethical rigorism—a revision which could follow from the thought that a legal proceeding which issues only from the guilt of the accused, without taking into account the influence of the world around him, and whose severity excludes every improvement and reintegration of the condemned into society, can never be humanly just.

From Helmut Richter, *Franz Kafka—Werk und Entwurf.* Berlin: Ruetten und Loenig, 1962. Pp. 117–19. [Trans. S.C.] Reprinted by permission of the publisher. Copyright © 1962 by Ruetten und Loenig, Berlin.

Selected Bibliography

Works of Kafka Cited in this Text

A = *Amerika.* Frankfurt am Main: S. Fischer, 1953. *Amerika,* trans. Edwin Muir. New York: New Directions, 1946.

B = *Beschreibungen eines Kampfes. Novellen, Skizzen, Aphorismen aus dem Nachlass.* Frankfurt am Main: S. Fischer, 1953. *Description of a Struggle,* trans. Tania and James Stern. New York: Schocken Books, 1958.

Br = *Briefe, 1902–1924.* Frankfurt am Main: S. Fischer, 1958.

S = *Das Schloss.* Frankfurt am Main: S. Fischer, 1955. *The Castle,* trans. Willa and Edwin Muir, with additional material trans. Eithne Wilkins and Ernst Kaiser. New York: Alfred A. Knopf, 1954.

T = *Tagebücher, 1910–1923.* Frankfurt am Main: S. Fischer, 1951.

Diaries I = *The Diaries of Franz Kafka, 1910–1913,* trans. Joseph Kresh. New York: Schocken Books, 1949.

Diaries II = *The Diaries of Franz Kafka, 1914–1923,* trans. Martin Greenberg with the cooperation of Hannah Arendt. New York: Schocken Books, 1949.

E = *Erzählungen.* Frankfurt am Main: S. Fischer, 1946. *The Penal Colony: Stories and Short Pieces,* trans. Willa and Edwin Muir. New York: Schocken Books, 1948.

F = *Briefe an Felice.* Frankfurt am Main: S. Fischer, 1967.

H = *Hochzeitsvorbereitungen auf dem Lande und andere Prosa aus dem Nachlass*. Frankfurt am Main: S. Fischer, 1953. *Dearest Father: Stories and Other Writings*, trans. Ernst Kaiser and Eithne Wilkins. New York: Schocken Books, 1954.

P = *Der Prozess*. Frankfurt am Main: S. Fischer, 1953. *The Trial*, trans. Willa and Edwin Muir; revised, and with additional materials trans. E. M. Butler. New York: Random House (The Modern Library), 1957.

Works about *The Metamorphosis*

Adams, Robert M. *Strains of Discord: Studies in Literary Openness*. Ithaca, New York: Cornell University Press, 1958. Pp. 168-79.

Adorno, Theodor W. "Aufzeichnungen zu Kafka," in *Prismen: Kulturkritik und Gesellschaft*. Frankfurt am Main: Suhrkamp, 1955. Pp. 302–42. "Notes on Kafka," trans. Samuel and Shierry Weber, *Prisms*. London: Spearman, 1967. Pp. 245–72.

Anders, Günther. *Kafka—Pro und Contra*. Munich: Beck, 1951. *Franz Kafka*, trans. A. Steer and A. K. Thorlby. London: Bowes and Bowes, 1960.

Angus, Douglas. "Kafka's 'Metamorphosis' and 'The Beauty and the Beast' Tale." *Journal of English and Germanic Philology*, LII (Jan. 1954), pp. 69–71.

Baioni, Giuliano. *Kafka, Romanzo e parabola*. Milano: Feltrinelli, 1962. Pp. 81–100.

Beissner, Friedrich. *Der Erzähler Franz Kafka*. Stuttgart: Kohlhammer, 1952.

———. *Franz Kafka der Dichter*. Stuttgart: Kohlhammer, 1958.

Benjamin, Walter. "Franz Kafka. Zur zehnten Wiederkehr seines Todestages," in *Schriften, II*, ed. T. W. Adorno and Gretel Adorno. Frankfurt am Main: Suhrkamp, 1955. Pp. 196–228. "Franz Kafka. On the Tenth Anniversary of his Death," trans. Harry Zohn, in *Illuminations*, ed. Hannah Arendt. New York: Harcourt, Brace, 1968. Pp. 111–40.

Bense, Max. *Die Theorie Kafkas*. Cologne and Berlin: Kiepenheuer und Witsch, 1952.

Binder, Hartmut. *Motiv und Gestaltung bei Franz Kafka*. Bonn: Bouvier, 1966.

Binion, Rudolph. "What the Metamorphosis Means." *Symposium*, XV (Fall 1961), pp. 214–20.

Blanchot, Maurice. "Kafka et l'exigence de l'oeuvre," in *l'Espace littéraire*. Paris: Gallimard, 1955. "The Diaries: The Exigency of the Work of Art," trans. Lyall H. Powers, in *Franz Kafka Today*, ed. Angel Flores and Homer Swander. Madison: The University of Wisconsin Press, 1964. Pp. 195–220.

Brod, Max. *Über Franz Kafka: Franz Kafka–Eine Biographie*; *Franz Kafkas Glauben und Lehre; Verzweiflung und Erlösung im Werk Franz Kafkas*. Frankfurt am Main and Hamburg: Fischer Bücherei, 1966. *Franz Kafka–A Biography*, trans. G. Humphreys Roberts and Richard Winston. New York: Schocken Books, 1960.

Brück, Max von. "Versuch über Kafka," in *Der Sphinx ist nicht tot: Figuren*. Cologne and Berlin: Kiepenheuer und Witsch, 1956. Pp. 117–35.

Corngold, Stanley. "Kafka's *Die Verwandlung*: Metamorphosis of the Metaphor." *Mosaic*, III:4 (1970), pp. 91–106.

Dalmau Castañón, Wilfredo. "El caso clínico de Kafka en 'La Metamorfosis.'" *Cuadernos Hispanoamericanos* (Madrid), XXVII (March 1952), pp. 385–88.

Dentan, Michel. *Humour et création littéraire dans l'oeuvre de Kafka*. Geneva and Paris: Droz and Minard, 1961. Pp. 11–16.

Edel, Edmund. "*Franz Kafka: Die Verwandlung, Eine Auslegung*." *Wirkendes Wort*, VIII:4 (1957–58), pp. 217–26.

Empson, William. "*The Metamorphosis*"—a review. *The Nation*, CLXII (December 7, 1946), pp. 652–53.

Emrich, Wilhelm. *Franz Kafka*. Frankfurt am Main and Bonn: Athenäum, 1956. Pp. 115–27. *Franz Kafka: A Critical Study of his Writings*, trans. Sheema Z. Buehne. New York: Ungar, 1968. Pp. 132–48.

Erlich, Victor. "Gogol and Kafka: Note on 'Realism' and 'Surrealism,'" in *For Roman Jacobson: Essays on the Occasion of his Sixtieth Birthday*, ed. Morris Halle and others. The Hague: Mouton, 1956. Pp. 102–04.

Freedman, Ralph. "Kafka's Obscurity: The Illusion of Logic in Narrative." *Modern Fiction Studies*, VIII (Spring 1962), pp. 61–74.

Goldstein, Bluma. "The Wound in Stories by Kafka." *Germanic Review*, XLI (May 1966), pp. 206–14.

Greenberg, Martin. "Gregor Samsa and Modern Spirituality," in *The Terror of Art: Kafka and Modern Literature*. New York: Basic Books, 1968. Pp. 69–91.

Hasselblatt, Dieter. *Zauber und Logik. Eine Kafka Studie*. Cologne: Verlag Wissenschaft und Politik, 1964. Pp. 192–205.

Henel, Ingeborg. "Die Deutbarkeit von Kafkas Werken." *Zeitschrift für deutsche Philologie*, LXXXVI:2, pp. 250–66.

Hermsdorf, Klaus. *Kafka: Weltbild und Roman*. Berlin: Rütten und Loenig, 1961. P. 96.

Heselhaus, Clemens. "Kafkas Erzählformen." *Deutsche Vierteljahrszeitschrift für Literaturwissenschaft und Geistesgeschichte*, III (1952), pp. 353–76.

Hillmann, Heinz. *Franz Kafka: Dichtungstheorie und Dichtungsgestalt*. Bonn: Bouvier, 1964. Pp. 138–39.

Holland, Norman N. "Realism and Unrealism: Kafka's 'Metamorphosis.'" *Modern Fiction Studies*, IV (Summer 1958), pp. 143–50.

Honig, Edwin. *Dark Conceit: The Making of Allegory*. New York: Oxford, 1966. Pp. 63–68 and *passim*.

Janouch, Gustav. *Gespräche mit Kafka, erweiterte Ausgabe*. Frankfurt am Main: S. Fischer, 1968. *Conversations with Kafka: Notes and Reminiscences*, trans. Goronwy Rees, New York: New Directions, 1969.

Kaiser, Hellmuth. "Franz Kafkas Inferno: Eine psychologische Deutung seiner Strafphantasie." *Imago* (1931), pp. 41–104.

Kassel, Norbert. *Das Groteske bei Franz Kafka*. Munich: Wilhelm Fink, 1969. Pp. 153–69.

Kayser, Wolfgang. *Das Groteske: Seine Gestaltung in Malerei und Dichtung*. Oldenburg-Hamburg: Stalling, 1961. Pp. 160, 221.

Landsberg, Paul L. "Kafka et la 'Métamorphose.'" *Esprit*, LXXII (Sept. 1938), pp. 671–84. "The Metamorphosis," trans. Carolyn Muehlenberg, in *The Kafka Problem*, ed.

Angel Flores. New York: New Directions, 1946. Pp. 122–33.

Lawson, Richard H. "*Ungeheueres Ungeziefer* in Kafka's *Die Verwandlung.*" *German Quarterly*, XXXIII (May 1960), pp. 216–19.

Lecomte, Marcel. "Note sur Kafka et le rêve (*La Métamorphose*)," in *Rêve*, ed. André Breton. Paris: 1938. Pp. 61–62.

Loeb, Ernst. "Bedeutungswandel der Metamorphose bei Franz Kafka und E.T.A. Hoffman: Ein Vergleich." *The German Quarterly*, XXXV (Jan. 1962), pp. 47–59.

Luke, F. D. "The Metamorphosis," in *Franz Kafka Today*, ed. Angel Flores and Homer Swander. Madison, Wisconsin: The University of Wisconsin Press, 1964. Pp. 25–43.

Madden, William A. "A Myth of Mediation: Kafka's Metamorphosis." *Thought*, XXVI (Summer 1951), pp. 246–66.

Margolis, Joseph. "Kafka vs. Eudaimonia and Duty." *Philosophy and Phenomenological Research*, XIX (Sept. 1958), 27–42.

Pfeiffer, Johannes. "Über Franz Kafkas Novelle 'Die Verwandlung.'" *Sammlung*, XIV, pp. 297–302. "The Metamorphosis," trans. Ronald Gray, in *Kafka: A Collection of Critical Essays*, ed. Ronald Gray. Englewood Cliffs, N. J.: Prentice-Hall, 1962. Pp. 53–59.

Politzer, Heinz. *Franz Kafka: Parable and Paradox*. Ithaca, New York: Cornell University Press, 1962. Pp. 65–84.

Pongs, Hermann. "Franz Kafka: 'Die Verwandlung,' zwischen West und Ost," in *Dichtung im gespaltenen Deutschland*. Stuttgart: Union, 1966. Pp. 262–85.

Reiss, H. S. *Franz Kafka: Eine Betrachtung seines Werkes*. Heidelberg: Lambert Schneider, 1952. Pp. 37–41.

Richter, Helmut. *Franz Kafka: Werk und Entwurf*. Berlin: Ruetten and Loenig, 1962.

Schlingmann, Carsten. "Die Verwandlung—Eine Interpretation," in *Interpretationen zu Franz Kafka: Das Urteil, Die Verwandlung, Ein Landarzt, Kleine Prosastücke*. Munich: Oldenbourg, 1968. Pp. 81–105.

Schubiger, Jürg. *Franz Kafka: Die Verwandlung, Eine Interpretation*. Zurich and Freiburg i. Br.: Atlantis, 1969.

Sokel, Walter H. "Kafka's 'Metamorphosis': Rebellion and Punishment." *Monatshefte*, XLVIII (April–May 1956), pp. 203–14.

————. *Franz Kafka: Tragik und Ironie, Zur Struktur seiner Kunst*. Munich and Vienna: Albert Langen, Georg Müller, 1964. Pp. 77–103 and *passim*.

————. *Franz Kafka*. Columbia Essays on Modern Writers. New York and London: Columbia University Press, 1966.

Sonnenfeld, Marion. "Paralleles in *Novelle* und *Verwandlung*." *Symposium*, XIV (Fall 1960), 221–25.

Sparks, Kimberly. "Drei Schwarze Kaninchen: Zu einer Deutung der Zimmerherren in Kafkas 'Die Verwandlung.' " *Zeitschrift für deutsche Philologie*, LXXXIV (1965), pp. 73–82.

Spilka, Mark. "Kafka's Sources for The Metamorphosis." *Comparative Literature*, XI (Fall 1959), pp. 289–307.

————. *Dickens and Kafka: A Mutual Interpretation*. Bloomington, Indiana: Indiana University Press, 1963. Pp. 77–79, 252–54.

Starke, Ottomar. "Kafka und die Illustration." *Neue literarische Welt*, IX (May 10, 1953), p. 3.

Stekel, Wilhelm. *"Die Verwandlung,"* in *Psychosexueller Infantilismus*. Berlin, 1923. P. 263.

Tauber, Herbert. *Franz Kafka: Eine Deutung seiner Werke*. Zurich and New York: Oprecht, 1941. *Franz Kafka: An Interpretation of his Writings*, trans. G. Humphreys Roberts and Roger Senhouse. New Haven, Conn.: Yale University Press, 1948.

Taylor, Alexander. "The Waking: The Theme of Kafka's Metamorphosis." *Studies in Short Fiction*, II (Summer 1965), pp. 337–42.

Ulshöfer, Robert. "Entseelte Wirklichkeit in Franz Kafkas 'Verwandlung,' Die Wirklichkeitsauffassung in der modernen Prosadichtung." *Der Deutschunterricht*, I (1955), pp. 27–36.

Webster, Peter Dow. "Franz Kafka's 'Metamorphosis' as Death and Resurrection Fantasy." *American Imago*, XVI (Winter 1959), pp. 349–65.

Weinberg, Kurt. *Kafkas Dichtungen: Die Travestien des Mythos.* Bern-Munich: Franke, 1963. Pp. 235–317.

Wiese, Benno von. "Franz Kafka: *Die Verwandlung,*" *Die deutsche Novelle von Goethe bis Kafka,* Vol. 2. Düsseldorf: Bagel, 1962. Pp. 319–45.

ABOUT THE AUTHOR

STANLEY CORNGOLD was born in New York City. He received his B.A. from Columbia University and Ph.D. in Comparative Literature from Cornell. He has also attended London and Basel Universities, the latter on an ACLS grant.

He has edited the prose of Max Frisch, a noted German writer, and is the author of a forthcoming study of Kafka's *Metamorphosis* entitled *The Commentators' Despair*. He is currently Associate Professor of German at Princeton.